"Dr. Helena Stevens' text on university supervision is an invaluable contribution, offering both clarity and depth to an often complex process. Her work provides practical guidance while advancing critical conversations about best practices."

John Harrichand, *Associate Professor,*
Montclair State University

"The text addresses a critical gap in counselor education by providing a comprehensive, practice-informed examination of university supervision. Dr. Stevens thoughtfully engages the paradox of supervision training, offering theoretically grounded frameworks to guide faculty, coordinators, and supervisors in the design and delivery of practicum and internship courses. Both emerging and experienced counselor educators will find this text to be an indispensable resource for cultivating intentional, ethical, and effective fieldwork experiences that align with CACREP standards and advance the preparation of future counselors."

Tracie Rutherford-Self, *Associate Professor,*
Minnesota State University, Mankato

COORDINATION AND SUPERVISION IN COUNSELING TRAINING PROGRAMS

This text is the first of its kind and provides counselor educators and supervisors, who teach university-level practicum and internship courses in counselor preparation programs, with a comprehensive exploration and in-depth understanding of all the facets that govern and influence university supervision courses.

Readers will learn how supervision theory infuses into group settings, along with a thorough understanding of how group dynamics impact the group supervision experience for fieldwork students. Topics covered include legal and ethical issues that university supervisors, site supervisors, and interns encounter and need to be competent in addressing. Culturally responsive supervision is covered to prepare the university supervisor to employ cultural capacity when working with students and supervisors. Procedures and practices for assessment and evaluation of students holistically, as well as suggested best practices for designing and coordinating fieldwork experiences for students in diverse counseling identity areas, are covered.

Counselor educators and supervisors will find this book helpful as it offers a comprehensive foundation for coordinating and teaching university supervision experiences and courses.

Helena G. Stevens is a counselor educator, licensed professional counselor, and licensed school counselor with over a decade of experience in the fields of counseling, counselor education, and supervision.

COORDINATION AND SUPERVISION IN COUNSELING TRAINING PROGRAMS

HELENA G. STEVENS

Routledge
Taylor & Francis Group

NEW YORK AND LONDON

Designed cover image: Getty Images

First published 2026
by Routledge
605 Third Avenue, New York, NY 10158

and by Routledge
4 Park Square, Milton Park, Abingdon, Oxon, OX14 4RN

Routledge is an imprint of the Taylor & Francis Group, an informa business

© 2026 Helena G. Stevens

For Product Safety Concerns and Information please contact our EU representative GPSR@taylorandfrancis.com. Taylor & Francis Verlag GmbH, Kaufingerstraße 24, 80331 München, Germany.

ISBN: 9781032412047 (hbk)
ISBN: 9781032412030 (pbk)
ISBN: 9781003356776 (ebk)

DOI: 10.4324/9781003356776

Typeset in Galliard
by codeMantra

To those who did not believe in me, did not support me, and denigrated me to crush my spirit, this book is for you. This book is also dedicated to the brilliant students who reminded me of how invaluable my work was to them both personally and professionally. Lastly, this book is dedicated to future professionals. Know that you are cut out for this work and may this book serve as your aid.

CONTENTS

ACKNOWLEDGMENTS

I want to acknowledge Sophie Dracott and Amanda Savage from Routledge for their unwavering support and encouragement in completing this book. I acknowledge my husband and children for being my biggest champions. I also want to acknowledge my colleagues for being consultants and supporters during the writing of this book.

Introduction

Practicum and internship courses have been a staple of counselor preparation programs since the late 1970s. The seminal article published in 1974, *Standards for the Preparation of Counselors and Other Personnel Services Specialists* (Association for Counselor Education and Supervision), detailed the parameters for practicum and internship components. Since then, accreditation standards and expectations for fieldwork have transformed significantly, leading to what counselor educators and supervisors now utilize in the Council for the Accreditation of Counseling and Related Education Programs (CACREP) 2024 standards.

Contextualizing Fieldwork in Counselor Preparation Programs within CACREP Standards

Practicum and internship, or as this book joins them into the category of fieldwork, are indivisible elements of counselor preparation programs. The CACREP defines fieldwork as, "professional practice, which includes practicum and internship, provides for the application of theory and the development of counseling skills under supervision" (CACREP, 2016). While CACREP is considered a "gold standard" and even a requirement of programs for certain state licensure boards, one will also find non-CACREP-accredited programs utilizing fieldwork as a required program component. While only some state boards require CACREP accreditation to obtain licensure as a mental health, school, marriage and family, or rehabilitation counselor (to name a few), state licensing boards consistently require fieldwork as a requirement in counselor preparation programs to be licensure eligible. Therefore, in counselor preparation programs, and per CACREP or state licensing board standards, practicum

DOI: 10.4324/9781003356776-1

and internship courses are required to be delivered as part of the fulfillment of the fieldwork components. These courses are referred to as "supervision courses."

The plethora of available materials that focus on the practice of supervision, within many professional and theoretical contexts, seems never-ending. However, materials that provide depth on the topic of teaching and designing courses for fieldwork and thus supervising the experience within the faculty role in counseling programs are sparse. In alignment with professional accreditation standards for counselor preparation programs, CACREP will serve as a foundational framework for understanding the principles that underpin professional practice, fieldwork, practicum, and internship experiences.

In the following chapters, there is an in-depth overview provided for teaching supervision courses. The CACREP (2024) *Professional Practice* (fieldwork) expectations are the same across the varying entry level (master's) professional identities. The identities of master's level addiction, career, mental health, clinical rehabilitation, college counseling and student affairs, marriage couple and family, school, and doctoral counselor education and supervision each have their own specific set of *Specialized Practice Areas*. Consequently, the expectations associated with each counseling identity vary according to the distinct professional responsibilities assigned to those roles. Doctoral standards are uniquely different from master's level standards across specialized and practice areas. In the overview, insight is provided into some of the differences between the different professional counseling identities and how those differences inform coordination and supervision practices for fieldwork courses.

In a later chapter, a deeper dive into assessment is provided. Programs assess student performance during practicum and internship, as these are when students apply the learning they have acquired in counseling practice. When deciding what students should do or how to assess them, "practice-based" standards are a valid foundation for developing the course framework. With each professional identity's *Specialized Practice Areas* containing standards unique to the identity, fieldwork courses are a natural fit for what can be considered "practice-based" standards. In previous CACREP standards, the standards were divided between knowledge and skill focus. That division no longer exists in the 2024 standards.

Expectations across Fieldwork Levels

Questions that arise for university supervisors may include "what should students be doing," or "what should I expect from students." From practicum through internship, from master's to doctoral, that question is answered differently, and in subsequent chapters, that answer is expanded upon. Practicum can be viewed as the building block period. Some students, up to this point, may have had zero experience or exposure to the population they intend to work with in the future. Likewise, not every student at the master's level will have an undergraduate degree or working experience in a human relationship field. This may be because it is neither an accreditation requirement nor is it frequently an admissions requirement. Also, a bachelor's degree in counseling is uncommon.

Doctoral students, who will only complete an internship, may encounter teaching and supervision as part of their professional practice for the first time, which is a key difference from master's programs. Certainly, there will be both master's and doctoral students who have had experience in practice areas in addition to students with zero practice experience. Therefore, practicum for master's students can be viewed as "first exposure" with an emphasis on how to make contact: building relationships, basic skills, and beginning conceptualization for the specific practice areas as they relate to the identity. Doctoral programs will consider the nuance of not having a practicum, first exposure element, and how to support students with limited to no experience in their internship work.

Internships, both developmentally and sequentially for master's students, are the next step. While CACREP (2024) does not delineate which *Specialized Practice* standards need to be addressed in practicum or internship, nor do the fieldwork requirements for professional practice detail the developmental difference for practicum and internship, this stage can be conceptualized as the opportunity to practice more advanced skills: assessment, treatment planning, larger system program management, consultation, to name a few. This stage may be anywhere from 1 to 3 (or more) semesters/quarters, depending on the program sequence design. As other chapters will expand more on these concepts, an important starting place is to be aware that there are developmental, practice, and assessment differences between practicum and internship. This notion influences other significant areas: placements, supervision, teaching, and coursework.

Training Opportunities for Counselor Educators

Just as with the array of teaching philosophies, pedagogical approaches, and learning theories, there are multiple methods for teaching fieldwork courses or designing fieldwork programs. The framework of this book is on the role of the university supervisor, with considerations for coordinators, who teaches and supervises counseling interns in counselor preparation programs. The purpose is to provide insight into methods and important considerations for the roles of fieldwork coordinator and university supervisors for both beginning and experienced counselor educators, adjuncts, professional counselors, and doctoral teaching assistants to have a solidified resource to utilize. As it currently stands, there is not one comprehensive resource. Additionally, in this book, we give attention to both master's and doctoral programs, with more emphasis on master's level programs in certain components.

There are books geared toward interns with some regard to supervisors, such as *The Internship, Practicum and Field Placement Handbook* (Baird & Mollen, 2023), *Practicum and Internship: Textbook and Resource Guide for Counseling and Psychotherapy* (Jungers et al., 2024), and *The Counseling Practicum and Internship Manual* (Hodges, 2024). Books such as *The Handbook of Counselor Preparation* (2010) and *Evaluation Student Learning Outcomes in Counselor Education* (2016) provide chapters specifically focusing constructivist pedagogy and assessment procedures. These books are nearly a decade to over a decade old and have no current updates despite the evolving nature of the accreditation standards that these texts are based on.

A search query for outcome research on student experiences in practicum courses will yield a high search return. Likewise, a search on the outcome research and conceptual literature (books and peer-reviewed articles) about clinical supervision and related areas of supervision will also yield a plethora of findings. A search on "how to teach practicum and internship counseling courses" will not yield many scholarly findings. While counseling, education, and supervision conferences provide a sampling of sessions on methods, assessment procedures, outcomes, and other related topics associated with fieldwork and practice, these sessions may be anecdotal, narrow, or inadequate guides for faculty and supervisors teaching and coordinating fieldwork experiences. At the risk of being repetitive, this book is focused on addressing the gap in training and conceptual materials to support the comprehensive work done by coordinators and university supervisors.

Nuances in Supervisor Requirements

Overview

In the academic setting, counselor preparation programs require university supervision courses, in tandem with the fieldwork being completed outside of the program, to fulfill accreditation requirements (CACREP, 2024). Decisions on who will teach are made departmentally by each program, as there is not one requirement as to whom is required to teach the university supervision courses, but rather accreditation standards provide guidance on who can teach. The 2024 CACREP practice standards have been updated in several ways from previous standards, ranging from changes in hour requirements, supervisor qualifications, and program requirements. However, in the entire section, there is no emphasis on the comprehensive scope of teaching the course nor on the coordination of fieldwork programs at a program systems level. While the standards are evolving and being enhanced, there are still areas for improvement.

CACREP (2024) standards for master's level counseling programs provide requirements for supervisors who provide individual/triadic and group supervision during practicum and internship. The individual providing individual, triadic, or group supervision may be the fieldwork site supervisor (potentially an adjunct), a core faculty member, or an affiliate faculty member. At the fieldwork site level, those individuals will need a minimum of master's degree, active certifications or licenses, a minimum of two years post-master's experience in the specialized practice area, relevant supervision training, and a knowledge of the program's expectations. At the university level, for group supervision, a core faculty member will have a terminal degree in counselor education and supervision. Affiliate faculty providing individual/triadic or group supervision must have relevant certifications or licenses and relevant training. Affiliate faculty may have degrees in other similar disciplines but are not required to have a doctoral degree. Doctoral students who are serving as individual/triadic or group supervisors must also have a master's degree, have completed or be completing supervision training and education, and be under the supervision of a qualified core or affiliate program faculty supervisor.

The master's level practice standards require students in practicum and internship to receive group supervision from either a program faculty or a doctoral student who is under the supervision of a core or affiliate program faculty member. Based on the description for supervisor requirements, a program faculty or doctoral student may be a site supervisor or provide the individual/triadic supervision, in addition to group supervision. Doctoral students will complete only an internship and are required to receive individual or triadic supervision. Doctoral practice standards also dictate that students are to receive group supervision from a core or affiliate program member. Like with master's level standards, that person may also provide individual or triadic supervision and is required to have relevant certifications and/or licenses and have completed specific sets of training.

Nuances

The master's level language used in this directive can be confusing, given that the first requirement is that the group supervision, usually provided in a course, should be provided by a program faculty. The second option is for a doctoral student who is under the supervision of a program or affiliate faculty, which leads one to believe that affiliate faculty could also teach a fieldwork course. Doctoral-level standards also indicate that an affiliate faculty can provide group supervision, also usually delivered in a course. Affiliate faculty, however, can be from a different discipline without a doctoral degree. Although affiliate faculty must be licensed and have supervision training, the variances from outside disciplines are significant and present a cause for concern.

In the master's level CACREP (2024) training standards, the singular standard in *Professional Counseling Orientation and Ethical Practice* states, "the purpose of and the role of counseling supervision in the profession" (pg. 12). A master's level clinician could serve as a fieldwork site supervisor and potentially a university supervisor as an affiliate faculty. There is an incongruence with the CACREP (2024) standards, requiring relevant training in supervision but not requiring it as a part of the standards at the master's level. Additionally, the standards do not specifically state what evidence or documentation must be collected (license, certification, continuing education credits, etc.). Therefore, outside training is required which leaves enough variability for concern on the reliability and validity of the external training. Additionally, while the *Professional Practice* section identifies that core and affiliate faculty need relevant training, that doctoral-level students are either concurrently enrolled in or have completed supervision preparation, there is no contextualization of what "relevant" means or identified standards for training to prepare for university-level teaching and supervision.

CACREP (2024) standards for doctoral counselor education and supervision programs do contain standards for supervision training and education. The supervision section in the 2024 standards lists 12 different categories of focus related to clinical supervision. Absent from these standards is emphasis specific to the role of university supervisor, group supervision, coordination of fieldwork programs, and any other wording that might lead a faculty down the avenue to consider training or education for doctoral students to be able to teach a practicum or internship course in the future. The reliance on supervision training in a course is a faulty foundation for ensuring that future university-level supervisors are properly prepared and competent to execute the dynamic and complex role that they will be tasked with. Additionally, with counselor education doctoral programs typically covering supervision standards in a supervision course, affiliate faculty who do not have doctoral degrees may have never taken a supervision course or received graduate program-level supervision training.

The Paradox

There appears to be a paradox. Master's level courses do not train for supervision, as there is no body of standards requiring programs to do so. Not every counseling identity requires post-master's level training on supervision to work at a supervisor's level (i.e. school counseling, college student affairs). Not every licensed individual will embark on supervision training because becoming a supervisor is not always required for their professional work. Additionally, supervision training can be lacking in emphasis on supervision in group or university settings. Counselors from varying identities at the master's level who do not require advanced training leading toward a supervisor license or state board approved supervisor credential could become instructors of practicum and internship courses. While the standards espouse having relevant training, the directive is not clear on what constitutes relevant or where the training needs to come from. There is no guidance on what evidence needs to be collected, on authenticating the training, or determining its validity.

For the set of standards in doctoral CES programs, a class is traditionally offered, and the emphasis on future professional work can vary.

Potentially, a student will have had zero engagement or exposure to supervision prior to taking this class and may not receive training on how to teach a practicum or internship courses, how to coordinate fieldwork programs, or what entails group supervision at a university level beyond the one chapter they read in a textbook. Yet, they are likely to teach either or both courses upon beginning a faculty role in a counselor preparation program.

Purpose of the Book

As you read this introduction, you may find yourself relating greatly to the paradox or you may be asking yourself, so what are we supposed to do? Typically, new and seasoned faculty (university supervisors) find themselves doing what has been done before them: adopting the same syllabi and pedagogical practices, being mentored by colleagues who come from the same training paradox, and attending conferences to get more training and education on supervision and fieldwork topics. In the end, this author believes that we all try to do our best to throw something together that feels efficient, ethical, intentional, and honors the CACREP standards for students as programs seek to obtain or maintain their accreditation status.

The intention is not to demoralize the standards. This author firmly believes programs need guiding principles for our education and training approaches. The inspiration for this text came from the many years spent struggling to figure out exactly what the author was supposed to be doing in the practicum and internship courses she taught. The purpose of this book is to provide guidelines for faculty and supervisors who come from the same paradox training world so that programs can provide intentional, grounded, and ethical fieldwork experiences and supervision courses.

It cannot be asserted for all doctoral supervision courses at every doctoral counselor education and supervision program, but it is reasonable to assume that many are similar to the one the author experienced. There was a strong emphasis on 1:1 clinical supervision, an opportunity to supervise a master's level student, opportunities but not requirements for co-teaching master's level fieldwork courses, and the adoption of the widely used, and often referenced in this textbook, *Fundamentals of Clinical Supervision* (Bernard & Goodyear, 2019) text.

The author was not fortunate enough to have positive and supportive mentoring when she entered the field of academia. There was no text to fall back on to help understand what she was supposed to be doing in her faculty, coordinator, and university supervisor roles. Simply applying what had been done before did not work for her teaching style or supervision philosophy. Yet, she was expected to do just that and consistently told (despite positive student evaluations) that she was bad at it. Therefore, she ended up hating teaching fieldwork classes and hating supervision.

Personal Anecdote

I can remember the day where "it" all clicked for me, when I finally understood what "it" was about, and what I could be doing. I realized all the capacity and opportunity I had, and because of that I began to love "it" and love supervision. I put "it" into quotations because it will take the entire book to explain "it." That is my rationale for this book. University supervision courses are bigger than an article, bigger than a chapter, and bigger than a conference presentation. This book is going to break "it" down so that the reader can walk away with a deeper understanding of the interconnected facets of university supervision courses, the role of the university supervisor, and how to coordinate fieldwork programs. Because many new faculty are asked to do this, as they exit the paradox, a framework and guidelines are crucial. This book is not meant to bind you into one lane of a framework. Rather, it is meant to help you understand all about what "it" is that is going on in university supervision courses and what options you have to deliberately engage in your role as university supervisor.

Note about Charts, Tables, and Decision-Making Guides

Throughout the book, readers will encounter charts, tables, decision-making guides, and frameworks associated with the chapters' contents. These items were all created by the author of this book with considerations for accreditation standards and research espoused practices or outcomes, as relevant to the content area. They were created to bridge theory into practice, specify supportive behaviors and attitudes, and provide tangible resources for professional practices.

Conclusion

This introduction broaches the paradox between supervision training and teaching university supervision courses. This book will support not only beginning faculty and supervisors but experienced professionals. This book dives deeper into designing fieldwork sequences, teaching, and assessment, and further into areas of group dynamics, culturally responsive practices, ethical, and development considerations. Professionals will now have a seminal resource to guide their professional practice to contribute to intentional practices that increase efficacy in the practice training of pre-service counselors and counselor educators.

References

Association for Counselor Education and Supervision. (1974). *Standards for the preparation of counselors and other personnel services specialists.* Washington, DC: Author.

Baird, B. B., & Mollen, D. (2023). *The internship, practicum, and field placement handbook: A guide for the helping professions* (9th ed.). New York, NY: Routledge.

Bernard, J. M., & Goodyear, R. K. (2019). *Fundamentals of clinical supervision* (6th ed.). New York, NY: Pearson.

Council on Accreditation of Counseling Related Education Programs. (2024). *2024 CACREP Standards.* Retrieved from https://www.cacrep.org/wp-content/uploads/2023/12/2024-CACREP-Standards.pdf

Council on Accreditation of Counseling Related Education Programs. (2016). *2016 CACREP Standards.* Retrieved from https://www.cacrep.org/for-programs/2016-cacrep-standards/

Hodges, S. (2024). *The counseling practicum and internship manual: A resource for graduate counseling students in a dynamic global era* (4th ed.). New York, NY: Springer.

Jungers, C. M., Scott, J., & Gregoire, J. (2024). *Practicum and internship textbook and resource guide for psychotherapy* (7th ed.). New York, NY: Routledge.

THE ROLE OF THE UNIVERSITY SUPERVISOR IN COUNSELOR EDUCATION PROGRAMS

Abstract

The profession of counselor education and supervision is a complex and challenging entity. The goal is to guide students toward excellence in their future counseling work. Faculty who work in these programs are tasked with creating programs and courses that are academically rigorous, adhere to accreditation standards, cross-culturally relevant, and inclusive of experiential learning experiences that deepen engagement with the complex intersections of human development, multiculturalism, societal systems, and their impact on mental health. At the heart of a counseling training program is the fieldwork experience. Practicum and internship are when students (interns) put the learning they've received to task in their direct and indirect counseling work. Therefore, the university supervisor, the faculty who teaches and supervises the fieldwork courses, is an essential and fundamental figure who influences and shapes the professional and personal developmental experiences of the students. This chapter will introduce the roles and responsibilities that a university supervisor has.

Roles of the University Supervisor

University supervisors, also regarded as faculty—whether designated as core or affiliate or employed adjunct or full-time position—undertake a wide-ranging array of roles and responsibilities in their work. Each role is pivotal to the success of students and counselor preparation programs. Those roles include teacher, supervisor, mentor, advocate, and leader. At the crux of the role is the relationship between the university supervisor and both the individual student and the supervision group. The responsibilities include fostering professional and personal growth, gatekeeping, ensuring ethical and legal compliance, and supervision work that will monitor and

DOI: 10.4324/9781003356776-2

11

guide counseling skill development and competencies. Wellness is both a philosophy and a practice that a university supervisor deliberately attends to in all aspects of their work. Additionally, university supervisors are a liaison between fieldwork program coordinators, fieldwork sites, and site supervisors. Thus, the university supervisor operates in a dynamic role to facilitate one of the most critical parts of counseling training.

Per CACREP (2024) standards, university supervisors should have training in supervision. Typically, individuals in these roles have advanced clinical experience, a professional identity in the field for which the counseling program specializes, and a terminal degree in counselor education and supervision from an accredited program. It is possible for affiliate faculty from various disciplines, doctoral students who have minimal experience, and first-year faculty with limited clinical backgrounds and only one semester of supervision coursework from their doctoral studies to teach a supervision course.

A solidified identity as a university supervisor, comprised of the array of roles, with an awareness of all the responsibilities included in the roles, can be lacking. Regardless of the readers' professional identity or role, this chapter will assist in building an integrated identity with the inherent and essential roles of a university supervisor. The book will further address each of these roles in depth.

Teacher

The university supervisor is the faculty of record for the practicum or internship course. Therefore, they are teachers. Teaching may feel like a secondary directive to supervision, but it is an inherent element in supervision. In the *Discrimination Supervision Model* Bernard (1997) explains that within supervision, teachers adopt a role to provide structure that includes, "instruction, modeling, and giving direct feedback" (Bernard & Goodyear, 2019, pg. 47). This conceptualization is congruent with teacher identity of a university supervisor and the core functions of a graduate-level counselor education faculty.

While not every supervision theory adopts the role of teaching, within the faculty identity is the directive to teach as needed. University supervisors consider the needs of students from a prescriptive and responsive approach. With knowledge and skill-based CACREP (2024) standards being imbedded in a supervision course, a faculty will consider the opportunities for teaching, modeling, or providing resources for learning the assigned standards prescriptively, before teaching the supervision course. Responsive teaching approaches are guided by observations, discussions in and outside of the supervision course, review of skills (live or recorded), and consultation with interns, site supervisors, or program coordinators. Assessment and evaluation of progress, another teaching directive, is habitual and continuous. Assessment practices happen before students enter their fieldwork phase and throughout the entirety of it. Therefore, faculty must continuously monitor the individuals' and group's progress and competency building to determine the teaching opportunities and responsibilities.

Supervisor

It goes without saying, a university supervisor is a supervisor. They pull from supervision theories and models that are relevant and responsive to the needs of the students and goals of the program. Those approaches are developmental, person-centered, psychoanalytical, or integrated. The most used text in doctoral level programs and supervision training is *Fundamentals of Clinical Supervision* (2019) by Janine Bernard and Rodney Goodyear. Additional books include *The New Handbook of Counseling Supervision* (Border & Brown, 2022), *Clinical Supervision: A Competency Based Approach* (Falender & Shafranske, 2021), *Essentials of Clinical Supervision* (Campbell, 2006), *Clinical Supervision in the Helping Professionals: A Practical Guide* (Corey et al., 2021), and *Practical Approaches to Clinical Supervision across Settings* (Lenz & Flamez, 2021). These resources are infused throughout the book with a primary utilization of the Bernard and Goodyear (2019) text. Faculty can find supplemental training at state and national conferences, in additional books and print materials, as well as online via webinars and virtual training.

Supervision is indivisible from counseling training programs. It is vital for the intern who is preparing for their future professional work. The fieldwork phase is sensitive, vulnerable, exciting, and at times terrifying for interns. The university supervisor's work has the capacity to make or break an intern's passage from learning to action. University supervisors must uphold the highest standards for supervision practice, ethical behaviors, culturally responsive supervision, and mentoring. The ways in which feedback, support, consultation, and instruction are delivered will substantially influence an intern's self-efficacy, competence, and confidence as they transition into the profession. Therefore, a university supervisor is responsible for building supportive relationships with the individuals and supervision groups to leverage the critical elements of supervision and lead interns toward growth and increased self-efficacy.

Mentor

As teachers and supervisors, faculty will impact knowledge, foster skill development, and aid in competency building. With the imperative to build supportive relationships and build safe and trusting environments in group supervision, mentoring is essential in that work. Mentoring is beyond knowledge building and focuses on empowering interns toward growing and reaching their potential. This work is less prescriptive and more focused on responding to the unique needs and personalities of interns. The mentoring can also be done with the whole supervision group, not just the individual. It can happen in the classroom and outside of the classroom when appropriate via individual meetings. While there may be overlaps between supervision and mentoring, mentoring work is characterized by a mutual intentional and increased levels of involvement with the intern that extend beyond the typical parameters of supervision work (Johnson, 2014; Bogwu, 2020).

As mentors, faculty lean into their counseling skills. Recent research highlights the significance of authentic mentoring relationships in counselor education. For example, Magnuson et al. (2022) highlighted that mentoring founded on mutuality and trust can foster greater counselor self-efficacy and professional identity development. With mentoring relationships being less transactional and focused on a mutual engagement that works toward transformation or growth, faculty utilize core therapeutic conditions, such as empathy, unconditional positive regard, and the creation of a safe environment for interns to share their struggles (Bogwu, 2020; Johnson, 2014).

As supervisors set high standards and expectations, the integration of empathy during constructive feedback, evaluation, and consultation helps mitigate power dynamics and supports a partnership that promotes positive professional growth (Bernard & Goodyear, 2019; Borders et al., 2023). Faculty may use self-disclosure and immediacy to show support and strengthen the supervisory alliance, with recent studies (Borders et al., 2023) emphasizing the role of authenticity in building effective supervisory relationships. Ultimately, effective mentoring in supervision nurtures transformative growth, empowering interns to realize their full potential as future counselors.

Advocacy

This dimension requires concerted attention. Recent literature highlights that while teaching interns advocacy skills is fundamental, supervisors themselves must also embody advocacy in their roles (Dollarhide et al., 2022). Supervisors act as advocates, leveraging their authority to ensure interns voices are heard and their concerns addressed—a practice increasingly recognized as crucial not only for intern well-being but also for the quality of client care (Magnuson et al., 2022). As intermediaries between sites, site supervisors, and program coordinators, university supervisors occupy a unique vantage point to support and empower interns, particularly when power dynamics might otherwise silence them (Borders et al., 2023). University supervisors must remember not only how vulnerable interns are but also that the power dynamics between interns and their superiors can end up silencing interns when they are experiencing negative circumstances.

Interns inevitably encounter unfair or unethical practices, inequities, mental health challenges, financial barriers, and other invisible hurdles that can hinder their growth. Research emphasizes the supervisor's role in advocating fair evaluation, equal learning opportunities, and access to resources (Borders et al., 2023). In navigating ethical "gray areas," supervisors demonstrate advocacy and social justice behaviors that interns are encouraged to adopt in their future practice (Dollarhide et al., 2022). Modeling advocacy in this way is shown to foster intern self-efficacy, professional identity, and resilience (Magnuson et al., 2022).

The advocacy work is not solely and directly for the interns but also for the clients the interns are working with. Supervisors consider teaching interns how they are advocates for client welfare, their impact on policy change to improve systems that impact mental health, and their role for intervening against injustice (Glosoff & Durham, 2010). This is highly sensitive work, and university supervisors need to seek supplemental training on infusing social justice and advocacy work into their clinical supervision work.

Leadership

University supervisors are multifaceted leaders. Their identity is grounded in being a group leader, much like a group counselor. This identity moves away from didactic approaches, whether teaching, supervising, or mentoring, and into a collective approach that is inclusive of everyone in the group. While there are certainly moments in supervision courses where the attention is 1:1, group leaders never stop attending to the group as a whole. University supervisors conceptualize that the productivity, growth, and success of the supervision course is dependent upon the cohesion and functioning of the group, which is indivisible from the group leader's work.

Leadership is essential to the mentoring and guidance work of supervisors. With an identity rooted in cultivating, inspiring, and fostering growth and empowerment in interns, leadership is non-negotiable for university supervisors. Therefore, they will work collaboratively with not only interns but also key stakeholders who impact the internship experience. Ethical dilemmas, crises, burnout, vicarious trauma, marginalization, and even more barriers will come up for interns along their developmental journeys. University supervisors will act as leaders to be the stable home base for interns to turn to, to receive guidance, instruction, advocacy, gatekeeping, and support.

Wellness

Wellness in the context of counseling internship is a holistic concept. It encompasses physical, emotional, social, intellectual, and spiritual dimensions. Interns often face unique stressors, including high client caseloads, emotional labor, ethical dilemmas, financial constraints, role ambiguity, existing mental health concerns, isolation, self-doubts, and the struggle to balance academic responsibilities with personal life. Unchecked, these stressors can lead to burnout, compassion fatigue, and even attrition from the field. As such, the wellness of counseling interns is not merely an ancillary concern—it is foundational to their professional development, ethical practice, and long-term career sustainability.

Emphasis on wellness is paramount for ethical counseling training programs (Roberts, 2019). In recognition of the significant influence that university supervisors hold, wellness should be embedded into the mentoring, leadership, and advocacy work (Garcia & Thomas, 2022). University supervisors are ideally positioned to promote wellness, fostering growth and resilience in interns (Kim & Jordan, 2015). We espouse that wellness should be a pillar in the framework of all counselor preparation programs and be even more visible in the supervision work during fieldwork.

University supervisors take on the responsibility to be a catalyst for inspiring interns, both in the work they bring into supervision and the role modeling of their own wellness practices, to engage in healthy behaviors that will, in turn, help create a healthier profession in the future (Evans & Brooks, 2018). Practices in courses can include integrating wellness modules into supervision curricula, offering resources for self-care, and encouraging a culture of mutual support (Hernandez et al., 2020). This is done through the mentoring work that centers on empathic relationships and utilization of reflective practices in supervision. The emphasis is on helping interns thrive through difficulties and on building habits that they will take into their future careers.

University supervisors must develop a framework to utilize as they are vigilant for signs of burnout, compassion fatigue, and vicarious trauma in interns (Smith & Lee, 2019). There is a fine line between the role of university supervisor and a professional counselor (Martinez & Chen, 2021), and university supervisors need to stay within their scope and be prepared with necessary resources when it is time to refer an intern to external support systems (Taylor & Nguyen, 2016). They can provide resources and access to appropriate services for interns throughout the fieldwork phase (Davis et al., 2020). They must also stay mindful of boundaries, confidentiality, and dual relationships (Brown, 2017).

We encourage further training in this area and in Table 1.1 we provide a visual guide for university supervisors as they promote wellness attitudes and behaviors in their work.

Table 1.1 Wellness Guidance

Practice	Description
Establish trust and rapport	Build a strong, supportive relationship at the outset of supervision.
Integrate wellness discussions	Regularly include self-care and wellness topics in supervision sessions.
Model healthy boundaries and stress management	Demonstrate effective stress management and maintain professional boundaries.
Encourage reflective practice	Promote journaling, case discussions, and debriefing to foster self-awareness.
Facilitate peer support	Support group supervision and collaborative activities among interns.
Remain vigilant for distress	Watch for signs of stress or burnout and intervene when needed.
Provide wellness resources	Share information about available resources and help interns access them.
Engage in ongoing development	Continually pursue professional development in wellness and supervision.

Envisioning the Role

This role involves complex dynamics that may present various challenges. Rather than concentrating initially on meeting specific standards within each area, the recommended starting point is to consider the central question: "Who will I be?" The roles are fluid, with less capacity to prescript who a supervisor will be in any given moment. As mentioned, there is a high degree of responsibility to be responsive to the professional, developmental, ethical, and legal challenges that arise. In those moments, a supervisor will always strive to "get it right." Before being able to do that, a supervisor needs to consider who they are as a person, counselor, teacher, and supervisor. Below are questions to consider. Readers are also encouraged to explore these questions with experienced university supervisors or other mentors whom they have a trusting relationship with.

- How has your understanding of the supervisor's role evolved as a result of reading this chapter?
- What personal and professional values guide your approach to supervision, mentorship, and advocacy?
- In what ways do you anticipate growing as a culturally responsive supervisor?
- How might you navigate ethical dilemmas that arise in your supervision practice?
- What strategies discussed in this chapter could you apply in your own development as a supervisor or faculty member?
- How do you envision building authentic connections with supervisees or students in group settings?
- What does "power and influence" mean to you in the context of supervision or mentorship?
- Are there aspects of your personal identity that may impact your approach to supervision or mentorship? How will you address them?
- What questions do you still have after engaging with this chapter?

We view answering these questions as challenging no matter what stage of career the reader is in, but also especially challenging in early career stages. Because the focus of this book is to add to the lack of resources available for faculty who are university supervisors, we advocate for starting with exploring the person of the faculty, supervisor, and counselor before diving into the behavioral work comprised of this role.

Conclusion

The university supervisor in counseling education programs wears many hats. Beyond supervision and teaching, they are mentors, advocates, and leaders. They view wellness as a pillar in the philosophy of their teaching and supervision work. Their impact begins in the classroom and continues long after interns have completed their programs. They influence not only skill development, but also self-efficacy, confidence, personal growth, and maturity. The sensitivity of the fieldwork experience demands that supervisors be dynamic and competent in all these aspects.

References

Bernard, J. M. (1997). The discrimination model. In C. E. Watkins (Ed.), *Handbook of psychotherapy supervision* (pp. 310–327). New York, NY: Wiley.

Bernard, J. M., & Goodyear, R. K. (2019). *Fundamentals of clinical supervision* (6th ed.). New York, NY: Pearson.

Bogwu, J. O. (2020). The importance of mentoring relationships independent of supervision for clinical psychology trainees. *Journal of Cognitive Psychotherapy: An International Quarterly, 34*(2), 99–106.

Border, L. D., & Brown, L. L. (2022). *The new handbook of counseling supervision* (1st ed.). New York, NY: Routledge.

Borders, L. D., Cashwell, C. S., & Giordano, A. L. (2023). *Supervision: A guide for the helping professions* (3rd ed.). Alexandria, VA: American Counseling Association.

Brown, T. (2017). Ethical supervision practices in counselor training. *Journal of Counseling Ethics, 12*(2), 45–58.

Campbell, J. M. (2006). *Fundamentals of clinical supervision* (1st ed.). Hoboken, NJ: Wiley.

Corey, G., Haynes, R., Moutlton, P., & Muratori, M. (2021). *Clinical supervision in the helping professions: A practical guide* (3rd ed.). Alexandria, VA: American Counseling Association.

Council for Accreditation of Counseling and Related Educational Programs (CACREP). (2024). 2024 Standards. https://www.cacrep.org/for-programs/2024-cacrep-standards/

Davis, R., Smith, J., & Lee, A. (2020). Wellness resources for counseling interns: Access and intervention. *Counselor Education Review, 28*(4), 211–224.

Dollarhide, C. T., Gibson, D. M., & Sagnik, B. (2022). Advocacy in counselor education: Current trends and future directions. *Journal of Counselor Preparation and Supervision, 15*(2), 45–62.

Evans, L., & Brooks, M. (2018). Thriving in counselor education: Supervisory advocacy and support. *Journal of Professional Counseling, 19*(3), 99–115.

Falender, C. A., & Shafranske, E. P. (2021). *Clinical supervision: A competency-based approach* (2nd ed.). Washington, DC: American Psychological Association.

Garcia, F., & Thomas, P. (2022). Wellness-focused supervisory training in counselor education. *International Journal of Counselor Education, 33*(1), 5–19.

Glosoff, H. L., & Durham, J. C. (2010). Using supervision to prepare social justice counseling advocates. *Counselor Education and Supervision, 50,* 116–129.

Hernandez, S., Kim, J., & Jordan, P. (2020). Fostering mutual support cultures in counselor education. *Educator's Forum, 14*(2), 77–89.

Johnson, W. B. (2014). Mentoring in psychology education and training: A mentoring relationship continuum model. In W. B. Johnson & N. J. Kaslow (Eds.), *The Oxford handbook of education and training in clinical psychology* (pp. 272–290). New York, NY: Oxford University Press.

Kim, J., & Jordan, P. (2015). Promoting holistic well-being in counselor supervision. *Journal of Counselor Development, 22*(1), 56–70.

Lenz, S. A., & Flamez, B. (2021). *Practical approaches to clinical supervision across settings.* Hoboken, NJ: Pearson.

Magnuson, S., Norem, K., & Wilcoxon, S. A. (2022). Mentoring in counselor education: Promoting professional identity and self-efficacy. *Journal of Counselor Education and Supervision, 61*(2), 145–160.

Martinez, L., & Chen, W. (2021). Supervisory boundaries and stress responses in counseling interns. *Counselor Education Quarterly, 30*(3), 130–144.

Roberts, G. (2019). Wellness as foundation in counselor preparation. *Professional Counseling Perspectives, 25*(4), 201–215.

Smith, J., & Lee, A. (2019). Recognizing burnout and intervening in counselor training. *Journal of Counseling Wellness, 15*(2), 59–72.

Taylor, F., & Nguyen, S. (2016). Referring interns and respecting autonomy in supervision. *Supervision Insights, 8*(3), 142–154.

CHAPTER 2
TEACHING SUPERVISION COURSES

Abstract

Teaching a practicum and/or internship course can be an assignment for any faculty at any point in their educator career. Depending on the time in which a faculty or university supervisor was trained or completed their terminal degree, the standards used to guide their education and experiences could vary significantly. Even programs using identical CACREP standards can vary greatly in their teaching methods and faculty roles for university supervision courses. Therefore, the focus of this chapter is to provide insight into suggested practices for any professional who teaches a university supervision course. Direction for designing these courses from an accreditation framework is provided. It is important to keep in mind that there are two foci in a practicum or internship course: teaching and supervision. Attention will be given to each separately while understanding the two inevitably overlap.

Designing the Supervision Course

Where do I begin? This is a completely reasonable question to ask when you are first assigned to teach a supervision course. It is important to recognize that it is not possible to know everything; this book provides additional information and context to support understanding. Feeling like you should "just know" whether self-imposed or externally imposed is not a solid foundation to start on. Reaching the final plateau of "knowing" is highly debatable in the work of supervision and teaching. This chapter is not espousing one right way of teaching and supervising the fieldwork course. Rather, the goal is to help build a firm foundation to start on.

Some programs may expect their faculty to replicate what has previously been done. Or, one may also find themselves in the position of

DOI: 10.4324/9781003356776-3

creating new courses or with creative freedom to change the course lay-out. It can be difficult for faculty to pinpoint the reasons behind a previous supervision course's design, given its evolving nature and limited scholarly resources. In either aspect, knowing the accreditation standards is also imperative for a starting point. Reference Section 4: Professional Practice in the 2024 CACREP standards for further content.

Before addressing course development, the author highlights an often-unseen factor influencing faculty teaching and supervision: job security pressure. Whether in a tenure track, clinical position, adjunct, visiting, or doctoral intern position, there is pressure to maintain status quo to keep one's job and/or secure tenure. That pressure leads faculty to act in ways that please their superiors. This may explain why a faculty might persist in delivering a course using previous methods, even if those approaches do not align with their teaching philosophy or if the course did not achieve its intended outcomes. Within the promised creative freedom of university-level teaching, there are still boundaries that can prevent the reader from utilizing what they learn in this book. There are few, if any, scholarly pieces that will be more important than job security. It is acknowledged that this book introduces approaches not previously addressed in other resources, and that factors such as department dynamics, faculty roles, and tenure considerations must also be considered when designing or teaching supervision courses.

CACREP (2024) Considerations

This chapter covers in-classroom topics, emphasizing accreditation requirements that affect teaching. The coordination chapter addresses clinical hour expectations and scheduling considerations within the course sequence.

Practicum students are required to participate in an average of one and a half hours of group supervision per week over a full academic term that is a minimum of eight weeks consistent with the academic calendar. Practicum will likely only be offered for one term during any of the potential terms—fall, spring, or summer. Internship students must also participate in an average of one and a half hours per week of group supervision on a regular schedule throughout the term. For the internship course, there is not a specific week requirement for the length of the term and internship could span more than one term (quarter, trimester, or semester) during any of the potential terms. Doctoral students complete only an internship, a change from previous CACREP standards which required a practicum. They also participate in an average of one and a half hours of group supervision per week.

Academic Considerations

Fieldwork courses most commonly are offered as three credit courses which translate (in most cases) to 50 minutes per credit hour. Despite that time division, three credit courses in graduate-level programs are typically offered in three-hour blocks with some classes being two hours and fifty minutes. As the faculty conceptualizes the course based on academic parameters and accreditation parameters, critical questions arise:

- Do I teach and supervise for just the required one or one and a half hours or do I teach and supervise for three hours?
- Do we deliver the class every other week and to maintain the required average hours and spend the whole three hours in class when we meet?
- Do we extend the typical allotted time of three hours and add live fieldwork components with live supervision?

Fully online, mostly asynchronous programs must determine how to handle live group supervision when courses lack scheduled meeting times. This chapter will give insight into possible directions for a faculty to go. At the same time, each department, program, and university have the final authority to answer any question posed or not posed in this section. Faculty are encouraged to explore answering this question with department chairs, program directors, and other key administrators involved to maintain positive collaborative working relationships.

Pedagogical Considerations

The day, time, and duration for the course might already be decided before a faculty receives their teaching assignment. Or, it can be decided up collectively and concurrently in individual, group, or department meetings. In either fashion, it will be decided upon before the term begins. After scheduling the supervision or fieldwork course, the next step is to plan how best to use the allotted time, whether it's ninety minutes or three hours. One and a half hours versus three hours of instructional time will dictate what opportunities are available. In subsequent chapters, we discuss group supervision models and what the models dictate for the "working time" in supervision. In this section, we will discuss pedagogy.

An important starting point for faculty is being aware of where students are in their program sequence. Accreditation standards do not have a requirement for when these courses land in the degree sequence. This means students may have completed all their coursework or be in the beginning to middle of coursework completion. The prior learning content acquired can influence the material that faculty incorporate when addressing standards, teaching skills, and evaluating performance. Before divulging deeper into pedagogical practices, there are areas of impact that any faculty should keep in mind as they design activities and "coursework"

1. Are students at their sites in the morning, afternoon, or evening?
2. Do students come straight from site to class, or do they have a break before class?
3. How many other classes are they taking?
4. What classes have they already taken and how does that inform where students are at developmentally with skills and knowledge?
5. Is this a cohort model or will students be on different course sequence tracks?
6. Are the students of the same professional identity or a mix of identities?
7. Is the internship full time or part time?
8. Which day of the week does supervision class fall on?

Students with part-time supervised internships attending class on Monday mornings will have a different classroom experience than those in full-time internships meeting on Wednesday evenings, even if both groups are enrolled full-time in the counseling program. These dynamics will affect the energy, affect, and engagement levels students have. When a faculty is picking between experiential, constructive, or transactional teaching approaches, they must also consider the way they meet students in the class. Faculty should ensure their pedagogical design aligns teaching and learning theory with students' individual and group dynamics to effectively engage them in supervision classes.

Pedagogy and Course Design

Case notes, quizzes, essays, recordings, discussion forums, what do I do? The buffet of assignment choices can seem never ending and confusing when deciding on which approaches will work best in a supervision focused course. A three-credit class presumes that there will be a minimum of two and a half hours of instruction time and around three hours of classwork completed outside of the course. CACREP (2024) provides some direction with specific requirements for audio/video recordings and/or live supervision of students' interactions with clients. Students must lead or co-lead a counseling or psychoeducational group in either internship or practicum. Students should have opportunities to become familiar with professional activities and resources, integrate and apply their knowledge (CACREP, 2024). These directives can inform decision-making regarding in-class and out-of-class assignments. The faculty will also need to determine whether or not internship hours are applied to outside class-work credit hour requirements to further decide whether additional assignments align with credit hour guidelines.

At this point in the chapter, the concept of teaching may still feel nebulous. Depending on the strength of the teaching preparation a faculty has had, course design may feel anywhere from exciting to overwhelming. Teaching theory may answer the "how do I do this" question, but it can be less helpful for designing other elements of the course. Therefore, to avoid getting lost in the array of options for choosing assignments, we will discuss an evidence-based approach for faculty, whether starting from scratch or utilizing pre-developed materials, when designing the course.

Backwards Learning Design

In graduate-level courses, students are typically assigned a textbook and proceed through one or more chapters each week, sometimes incorporating additional external materials. Classroom lecturing focused on the assigned content for the week with a sequential learning sequence starting with chapter one of the assigned text and proceeding until the end of the text. The assignments might have been linked to CACREP standards and could have matched the learning content sequence, but that was not always the case. This approach is still an opportunity, but researchers note that this approach leads toward passive learning, ineffective teaching strategies, and non-student-centered approaches (Reynolds & Kearns, 2017).

Backwards Learning Design is a student-centered approach that starts with the end in mind. Research consistently supports the efficacy of backwards learning design in promoting deeper student engagement and improved learning outcomes. Studies have shown that when instructors begin with clear learning objectives and align assessments and instructional activities to those goals, students are more likely to understand expectations and demonstrate mastery of key competencies. For example, Fink (2013) and Dolan and Collins (2015) found that backwards design fosters active learning, encourages critical thinking, and leads to more meaningful application of knowledge compared to traditional content-driven approaches. Furthermore, Reynolds and Kearns (2017) highlight that this student-centered method reduces passive learning and helps ensure that instructional time is focused on essential skills and knowledge, which is especially valuable in professional programs like counseling education. Overall, the research suggests that backwards learning design is an effective framework for enhancing both teaching and student achievement in higher education settings.

Effectively using backwards learning design involves starting with the desired student learning outcomes (SLOs) and then planning instruction and assessments that directly support those goals. In counseling education, faculty first clarify their teaching philosophy and learning objectives, then design experiences—such as individual and group counseling, case reviews, psychoeducation workshops, and creative experiential activities—that align with these outcomes. In this approach, which moves away from long lectures, non-deliberate approaches, and traditional testing procedures, students engage in active learning that allows them to practice skills to demonstrate their competencies and gain in vivo feedback and intentional assessment in class (Dolan & Collins, 2015; Fink, 2013). Because this framework includes in vivo and skill-based components, it lends itself effectively for use in supervision courses due to the use of live demonstrations and consultation in supervision courses.

Below is a breakdown of the steps (Reynolds & Kearns, 2017), and at the same time, readers need to consider additional training in using this method.

Phase 1: Determine the Desired Student- Learning Outcomes

In this step, faculty and/or programs will consider student-learning outcomes (SLOs). CACREP standards can be utilized as the SLOs of a program. Knowing the SLOs and starting with them as the end in mind will decrease happenstance or non-deliberate approaches when designing the learning activities and determining academic materials. PLOs are standards in addition to SLO's. *Section 2: Academic Quality* (CACREP, 2024) details that programs will develop PLO's that reflect "current knowledge and need related to counseling practice in a diverse, multicultural, and global society with marginalized populations." CACREP (2024) standards also require programs to contain key performance indicators (KPIs) as a part of their program frameworks. While PLOs and KPIs may be assessed in fieldwork courses, CACREP standards for learning most closely align with the SLO component of *Backwards Learning*, and our examples will utilize SLO's with CACREP standards

As mentioned, SLOs will likely be determined in advance and therefore, a faculty will already know what the desired SLOs of the supervision course will be. There is also not one requirement for which standards will go into the fieldwork courses. The author encourages the SLOs to be skill based as they align cohesively with fieldwork and its focus on demonstration of competencies.

Example of SLO's Based on CACREP (2024) Standards

Entry-Level Specialized Practice Areas, Clinical Mental Health Counseling
Section 5-C.4: intake interview, mental status evaluation, biopsychosocial history, mental health history, and psychological assessment for treatment planning and caseload management

Doctoral Standards Counselor Education and Supervision
Section 6-3.e: the use of technology in instructional design and program delivery types

---

Phase 2: Determine Acceptable Evidence

CACREP's (2024) guidance on using recordings and live demonstration significantly influences this portion. If fieldwork focuses on applying course content and demonstrating skills, research papers, quizzes, or exams may not be necessary. This is not to say these traditional elements cannot find their place within other assignment and evaluation pieces, but there is not a high relevance for them to be primary assessment approaches or evaluative evidence. With skill demonstration (whether a recording or live demonstrations) being a primary artifact, faculty will consider what rubrics, or evaluation measures they will use too. Lastly, faculty members should consistently reference established standards, current research, and pedagogical approaches when evaluating student progress and performance.

For a demonstration, there will be two parts evaluated with potentially two parts of evidence in the assessment or evaluation. The first part assessed is the requirements of the assignment. The faculty will determine what the parameters for the assignment portion are. Rubrics can be developed "in-house" to evaluate for assignment completion. The second part is the execution of skills and/or dispositions. While a faculty can develop a rubric for assessing skills, an evidence-based tool is already available with the Counselor Competencies Scale-Revised (CCS-R) (Lambie et al., 2016; Mullen et al., 2025). This evaluation tool assesses two areas on a five-point scale: counseling skills and therapeutic conditions and counseling dispositions and behaviors. Of note, while there are copies that can be found doing a web search, the tool is copyrighted and programs need to seek permission for systematic use.

The Counselor Competencies Scale-Revised (CCS-R) is an empirically validated tool for assessing counseling competencies. Studies have shown that the CCS-R possesses strong psychometric properties, including reliability and validity, when used to evaluate counseling skills and dispositions in graduate counselor education programs (Lambie et al., 2016; Mullen et al., 2025). The CCS-R has undergone rigorous development and refinement, with evidence supporting its use as a standardized measure that provides objective, actionable feedback for both students and faculty. Validation research indicates that the scale effectively differentiates levels of counselor competence and is aligned with professional standards such as those set forth by CACREP. Furthermore, the CCS-R's consistent use in program evaluation and student assessment highlights its credibility and utility in both formative and summative assessment contexts. Its alignment with accrediting body requirements and its empirical foundation makes it a preferred choice for counseling programs seeking reliable assessment tools.

Example Assignments: These Assignments Were Developed by the Author and Infuse Standards from Both CACREP (2024) and the CCS-R (Lambie et al., 2016)

1. (Master) CACREP SLO: *Section 5-C.4: intake interview, mental status evaluation, biopsychosocial history, mental health history, and psychological assessment for treatment planning and caseload management*

Assignment: Client Conceptualization Assignment

CCS-R (Lambie et al., 2016) 2.E: Record Keeping and Task Completion
This assignment gives interns the opportunity to engage in clinical behaviors that teach comprehensive case consultation. It also reinforces group-based consultation supervision in the practicum or internship course.

1. *Students will submit and present a PowerPoint overview of a current client, including*

   a. *Age*
   b. *Demographics and Cultural Background*
   c. *Bio-psycho-social-family history*
   d. *Mental Health History*
   e. *Psychological Assessment Report Data*
   f. *Diagnosis*
   g. *Intervention history and other pertinent information to analyze the case*
   h. *Treatment Plan Overview*
   i. *Presenting Issues*
   j. *Case Consultation Needs of Intern*

2. (Doctoral) CACREP SLO: *Section 6-3.e: the use of technology in instructional design and program delivery types*

Assignment: Demonstration of Teaching Skills

CCSR (Lambie et al., 2016) Part 1 I.1
This assignment provides doctoral students with the opportunity to demonstrate the skills in the standard and receive feedback from the faculty supervisor and supervision group.

1. *Students will present a recording of their teaching during the supervision course. The teaching demonstrated will reflect tenants of the standard.*

> 2. *Students will provide a copy of their teaching/lesson plan for the session with the use of technology components highlighted.*
> 3. *Students will present a ten-minute segment for the group to view in which they are utilizing technology in their content delivery.*
> 4. *Students identify supervision needs for teaching competencies.*

These are just two examples of how an SLO informs an assignment and two different methods for assessment.

Phase 3: Plan Learning Experiences and Instruction

During this phase, faculty members identify and articulate their teaching and learning philosophy. In this chapter, we will discuss teaching theories that compliment tenants of the fieldwork courses. Backwards learning design is strengthened by the use of diverse teaching methods and resources, including textbooks that bridge theory and practice, live demonstrations, and technology-enhanced instruction. This approach is supported by instructional frameworks that encourage active engagement, reflection, and adaptation to student needs, resulting in more effective and dynamic learning experiences for counseling interns.

Current research highlights the importance of integrating technology and experiential learning, as outlined by Crumb et al. (2018), McAuliffe and Eriksen (2011), and Villarreal-Davis et al. (2021), who emphasize learning by doing, reflective practice, and creative approaches to enhance competency. Crumb and colleagues (2018) outline the following objectives for internship experiences inside and outside of the classroom to enhance learning: individual and group counseling, weekly case reviews or treatment team meetings, clinical assessments, writing progress notes, psychoeducation workshops, and working with specialized populations. Due to the needs for case consultation, a faculty may not find much time for instructional learning or didactic processes, but it does not mean they cannot integrate these pieces. By grounding instructional planning in backwards design, faculty ensure that each activity and assessment builds toward meaningful skill development and prepares students for real-world practice (Table 2.1).

This chart summarizes how backwards design ensures that each instructional component is purposefully aligned with meaningful skill development and prepares students for real-world professional practice.

TABLE 2.1 Backwards Learning Design Guide

Step	Description	Key Considerations
1. Identify Desired Outcomes	Determine the learning goals, competencies, or standards students should achieve by the end of the unit or course.	Align outcomes with professional practice and student needs.
2. Determine Acceptable Evidence	Design assessments and performance tasks that will demonstrate whether students have met the desired outcomes.	Use diverse assessment methods, including technology-enhanced activities and reflective practice.
3. Plan Learning Experiences and Instruction	Develop instructional activities, resources, and teaching strategies that support students in achieving the outcomes.	Incorporate active engagement, experiential learning, and adapt to student needs.

Teaching Considerations

Traditional teaching styles can tend to be transactional. The faculty delivers the content; the students receive the content and then are assigned relevant or irrelevant tasks to assess if the content has been received. To suggest a transactional approach to supervision courses would be incongruent to the theoretical frameworks espoused in literature. The provided frameworks in this chapter essentially espouse the same directive: have students increase their counseling competency with methods that engage them with "doing" aspects of their professional identity. This is not to suggest there will never be "teaching" components. In supervision theory (to be addressed in subsequent chapters), teaching is a role within the developmental model. There will certainly be times when a faculty teaches content on laws, ethics, techniques, and models.

How a faculty chooses to teach should keep in mind the cognitions of comprehension, application, analysis, synthesis, and evaluation directives for the knowledge being given in the teaching (Kindsvatter et al., 2008). Basically, what are students going to do with the knowledge you give them beyond knowing? Ultimately, thoughtful course design, guided by both empirical frameworks and the lived experience of faculty, lays the foundation for dynamic, skill-centered learning that prepares counseling students for the multifaceted realities of professional practice.

Constructivism and Experientialism

In the singular text available for counselor educator preparation, the framework provided for teaching practicum and internship courses is constructivism (McAuliffe & Eriksen, 2011). The authors cite Schon's (1987) work, which reflects that we learn best by doing, not just by thinking. Schon provides direction for learning counseling by (a) doing, (b) interactions with others, and (c) exposure and immersion. McAuliffe and Eriksen reflect that, "learning by doing highlights the importance of reflection in action" (2011, pg. 243). To not do so reduces the impact of what students are learning.

The fieldwork experience is the enhancement of the theory—interns are in the "doing phase." How does this translate into a classroom (whether in person or virtual) experience? Within activities such as case studies, case consultation, supervision of live demonstrations, and group discussions of clinical cases are items that espouse a learn by doing in a classroom setting. The two examples provided in Section "CACREP (2024) Considerations" highlight how students learn actively and vicariously from group supervision. Additionally, if a faculty perceives a deficit in skills and competencies based on the demonstrations in the assignments, they can provide instruction, demonstrations, or materials on the standards and student learning outcomes.

Experiential learning theory is a holistic approach that includes cognitive and emotional emphasis on the student's learning experiences and processes. Villarreal-Davis and colleagues (2021) posit that the use of creative and expressive art activities is an impactful approach when operating within the experiential framework. Expressive art includes kinesthetic/sensory, perceptual/affective, and cognitive/symbolic based creative activities (Lusebrink et al., 2013). Expressive arts in counseling, broad base, have ample efficacy for their use. Activities in the creative experiential approach include bibliosupervision, psychodrama supervision, sand tray, play-based activities, and adventure-based supervision. In supervision, researchers note that a creative approach engages the cognitive and emotional parts of the brain and fosters creative thinking, comfort with risk taking, comfort with ambiguity, flexibility, and problem-solving skills (Binson & Lev-Wiesel, 2018; Lawrence et al., 2015). These noted personal qualities are qualities found in skilled counselors (Corey, 2024).

For online programs, the supervision will largely depend on the virtual platform being used: Moodle, Desire2Learn, Blackboard, Zoom, Google, Microsoft, are several options. Technology has provided unique opportunities for virtual-based programs to remain innovative and inclu-sive. As mentioned, the 2024 CACREP standards require supervision class to be a live, synchronous component. For online, and certainly face-to-face programs, experiential learning theory provides a framework to concep-tualize classroom time. Examples of utilizing creative arts and experien-tial learning in online settings include the use of digital creative writing, graphic arts and mindfulness activities, and art-based activities that promote expression. Faculty should be mindful that the use of artistic and creative approaches can have a positive impact, and due to the risk-taking nature of these approaches, they can also elicit anxiety, discomfort, inhibition, and fear from interns. Therefore, further training is needed as well as being sensitive to the feelings of comfort from using art or expression in interns.

Faculty may use Table 2.2 to select the most appropriate approach based on course goals, student readiness, and desired outcomes. Blend-ing both frameworks often provides the most robust learning environ-ment, supporting the development of both cognitive and emotional competencies in counseling interns.

TABLE 2.2 Pedagogical Guide

Decision Factor	Constructivist Approach	Experiential Learning Approach
Learning Objective	To promote reflection, critical thinking, and meaning-making through active engagement and knowledge construction.	To immerse students in real-life or simulated experiences, fostering skill development and emotional engagement.
Instructional Methods	Case studies, group supervision, collaborative projects, and class discussions.	Live demonstrations, creative/ expressive arts, role plays, and adventure-based activities.
Best Used When	Students need to connect theory to practice and develop personal meaning through interaction and reflection.	Students benefit from hands-on practice, emotional processing, and building comfort with ambiguity and risk-taking.
Potential Challenges	May require strong facilitation to ensure depth of reflection; risk of remaining abstract without application.	Can elicit anxiety or discomfort; requires sensitivity and additional training for faculty and students.
Technology Integration	Discussion boards, collaborative documents, virtual case analysis.	Digital creative writing, online art-based activities, virtual role plays, and supervision.
Assessment Methods	Reflective journals, peer feedback, case presentations.	Performance tasks, demonstration of skills, creative project submissions.

Textbooks

Textbooks serve as foundational tools in counseling internship courses, bridging theory, and hands-on practice. Selections often include texts such as *The Counseling Practicum and Internship Manual: A Resource for Graduate Counseling Students in a Dynamic Global Era* (Hodges, 2024), which provides structured guidance and scenarios reflective of real-life practicum and internship challenges. Another resource is *Practicum and Internship: A Handbook for Competent Counseling Practices* (Jackson-Cherry & Sterner, 2022), which covers a breadth of topics in professional counseling with a focus on aiding the intern in advancing their skills. For those seeking a deeper exploration of supervision, *Clinical Supervision in the Helping Professions: A Practical Guide* (Corey et al., 2020) blends theoretical perspectives with day-to-day supervisory strategies. *The Internship, Practicum and Field Placement Handbook: A Guide for Helping Professions* (Baird & Mollen, 2023) is written for helping professions broadly and can be helpful for both interns and supervisors to explore underrepresented topics that are addressed from a post COVID-19 pandemic era, with added emphasis on virtual considerations. Lastly, the *Practicum and Internship Textbook and Resource Guide for Counseling and Psychotherapy* (Jungers et al., 2024) covers a similar breadth of topics related to clinical practice and provides emphasis on the transition from practicum to internship for interns.

The thoughtful integration of these texts, paired with the instructor's professional insight and the activities embedded within the course, cultivates a learning environment that prepares students to move beyond classroom knowledge and into the realities of counseling practice. As with all instructional choices, the selection of textbooks should align with the course's learning objectives, accreditation standards, and the developmental needs of students as they progress through their professional journey.

Getting Started

Although faculty skills are often highlighted, it's important to also reflect on the question: "Who am I?" Teaching involves not only course delivery and tasks, but also the personal identity of the faculty member—as an individual, advisor, and supervisor. The following section offers planning resources for university supervisors for both course content and professional identity considerations.

Decision-Making Guide

The decision-making guide in Table 2.3 is designed to help supervision course instructors navigate foundational aspects of teaching, implement best practices, and support the development of both students and themselves. Drawing on the chapter's themes—supervision methodology, goal setting, professional development, and self-assessment—this guide offers a step-by-step framework to inform your supervisory practice. It was developed by the author.

Step 1: Clarify Your Supervision Methodology

- Reflect on your educational values and beliefs about supervision.
- Review established supervision models (e.g., developmental, integrative, psychodynamic) and select one that aligns with your teaching philosophy and the needs of your learners.
- Document your chosen approach, including rationale and anticipated outcomes.
- Prepare to adapt your methodology as the course progresses and as student needs evolve.

Step 2: Articulate Primary Goals

- Identify specific, measurable objectives for both students and the course overall.

TABLE 2.3 Course Layout Planning Chart

Planning Item	Details/Comments
Course Duration	How many weeks is the course?
Class Size	How many students are in the course?
Meeting Schedule	What day/time will the course meet?
Delivery Format	Is the course face-to-face, virtual or hybrid?
Student Discipline	What disciplines (mental health counseling, school counseling, addictions etc.) are the students in?
Program Sequence	Where are students at in their program sequence?
Assigned Standards	What standards are assigned to this course?
Assessments and Evaluations	What are the required assessments and evaluations?
Assignments and Standards	What assignments are connected to the standards?

- Ensure your goals align with current professional standards and best practices in your field.
- Consult with colleagues or reference authoritative texts to benchmark your objectives.
- Communicate these goals clearly to students at the outset of the course and revisit them regularly.

Step 3: Assess Learner and Course Needs

- Gather information on students' backgrounds, experiences, and expectations.
- Use formative assessments, questionnaires, and reflective exercises to identify areas for growth among your students.
- Adapt your supervision strategies to address identified needs and foster a supportive learning environment.

Step 4: Identify Your Areas for Professional Growth

- Engage in honest self-assessment regarding your strengths and areas for improvement as a supervisor.
- Seek feedback from peers, mentors, and students to inform your development.
- Set professional development goals and pursue relevant training, literature, or supervision to address growth areas.
- Document your progress and update your goals as necessary throughout the academic year.

Step 5: Establish Supervision of Your Supervision

- Identify who will provide you with supervision or mentorship in your own supervisory role.
- Schedule regular meetings for consultation, case discussion, and support.
- Use this supervision to reflect on challenges, celebrate successes, and ensure accountability in your teaching practice.

Step 6: Integrate Theory with Standards-Driven Practice

- Use the educational model provided in the chapter as a reference for infusing theory with standards-driven practice.
- Continuously evaluate the effectiveness of your supervision by comparing actual outcomes to your stated goals and established standards.

- Modify your approach as needed based on reflection, feedback, and new developments in the field.

Step 7: Encourage Ongoing Reflection and Adaptation

- Maintain a reflective journal or portfolio documenting significant decisions, challenges, and learning experiences.
- Promote a culture of feedback and adaptability among students and colleagues.
- Remain open to change and growth, modeling lifelong learning for your students.

Conclusion

This chapter provides an in-depth exploration of foundational aspects related to the teaching of supervision courses. An educational model is provided for the readers to consider how to infuse teaching theories with standards driven practices. Additionally, we encourage the articulation of primary goals for students and courses, underscoring the necessity of clear, measurable objectives that correspond with both best practices and the evolving needs of learners. Supervisors are encouraged to engage in critical self-assessment, identifying key areas of growth and development.

References

Baird, B. B., & Mollen, D. (2023). *The internship, practicum, and field placement handbook: A guide for the helping professions* (9th ed.). New York, NY: Routledge.

Binson, B., & Lev-Wiesel, R. (2018). Promoting person growth through experiential learning: The case of expressive arts therapy for lecturers in Thailand. *Frontiers in Psychology, 8*(2276), 1–12.

Corey, G. (2024). *Theory and practice of counseling and psychotherapy* (11th ed.). New York, NY: Cengage.

Corey, G., Haynes, R., Moulton, P., & Muratori, M. (2020). *Clinical supervision in helping professions: A practical guide* (3rd ed.). Alexandria, VA: American Counseling Association.

Council on Accreditation of Counseling Related Education Programs. (2024). *2024 CACREP Standards.* Retrieved from https://www.cacrep.org/wp-content/uploads/2023/12/2024-CACREP-Standards.pdf

Crumb, L. et al. (2018). An interprofessional internship model for training master's level social work and counseling students in higher education settings. *Journal of Human Behavior in the Social Environment, 28*(8), 1091–1096.

Dolan, E. L., & Collins, J. P. (2015). We must teach more effectively: Here are four ways to get started. *Molecular Biology of the Cell, 25,* 2151–2155.

Fink, D. L. (2013). *Creating significant learning experiences: An integrated approach to designing college courses.* San Francisco, CA: Jossey-Bass.

Hodges, S. (2024). *The counseling practicum and internship manual: A resource for graduate counseling students in a dynamic global era* (4th ed.). New York, NY: Springer.

Jackson-Cherry, L., & Sterner, W. (2022). *Practicum and internship: A handbook for competent counseling practices* (1st ed.). New York, NY: Pearson.

Jungers, C. M., Scott, J., & Gregoire, J. (2024). *Practicum and internship textbook and resource guide for psychotherapy* (7th ed.). New York, NY: Routledge.

Kindsvatter, A., Granello, D. H., & Duba, J. (2008). Cognitive techniques as a means for facilitating supervisee development. *Counselor Education and Supervision, 47*(3), 179–192.

Lambie, G. W., Mullen, P. R., Swank, J., & Blount, A. (2016). Counselor Competencies Scale- Revised (CCS-R). Retrieved from https://cpb-us-w2.wpmucdn.com/sites.stedwards.edu/dist/f/5295/files/2020/02/CCS-R-Practicum-Evaluation-11-15-2017-PDF.pdf

Lawrence, C., Foster, V., & Tieso, C. L. (2015). Creating creative clinicians: Incorporating creativity into counselor education. *Journal of Creativity in Mental Health, 10*(2), 166–180.

Lusebrink, V. B., Mārtinsone, K., & Dzilna-Šilova, I. (2013). The expressive therapies continuum (ETC): Interdisciplinary bases of the ETC. *International Journal of Art Therapy, 18*(2), 75–85.

McAuliffe, G., & Eriksen, K. (2011). *Handbook of counselor preparation: Constructivist, developmental, and experiential approaches.* Thousand Oaks, CA: Sage.

Mullen, P. R., Lambie, G. W., Poandl, M. M., Frawley, C., & Burgin, E. (2025). Analysis of the counseling competency scale-revised using trainees' self-assessment data. *Counseling Outcome Research and Evaluation, 16*(1), 24–38.

Reynolds, H. L., & Kearns, K. D. (2017). A planning tool for incorporating backward design, active learning, and authentic assessment in the college classroom. *College Teaching, 65*(1), 17–27.

Schon, D. A. (1987). *Education the reflective practitioner.* San Francisco, CA: Jossey-Bass.

Villarreal-Davis, C., Sartor, T. A., & McLean, L. (2021). Utilizing creativity to foster connection in online counseling supervision. *Journal of Creativity in Mental Health, 2,* 244–257.

Chapter 3
Student Development

Abstract

For counseling internship students, several foundational areas are essential to foster professional growth and effective practice. These include the cultivation of core technical and relational abilities, the development of personal insight and resilience, the demonstration of ethical and responsible behavior, the embrace of diverse perspectives, and the integration of authentic practitioner experiences. Supervisors are keenly aware of the clinical skill development needs of interns and the imperative to have them ready to practice independently post-program completion. This chapter explores the professional and personal areas that students need to develop for future success in counseling.

Skill Development

Counseling programs are accountable for students' future clients the moment a student is accepted into a counseling program. A degree in counseling, regardless of discipline, qualifies a student to enter the profession, uninhibited. Some professional identities will not require a license, and students will immediately begin their practice. Some will immediately gain licensure and not require any supervision, whereas some will require thousands of hours of supervised practice to gain licensure. Regardless of licensure needs, the degree assumes that students are ready to practice without risk of causing harm to clients or being ineffective in their work. Therefore, supervision of skills at the university level is distinct from supervision in the field post-degree, in that university supervisors have an arguably higher degree of responsibility to prepare interns for career readiness.

DOI: 10.4324/9781003356776-4

The development of counseling skills began before the students became interns. Introduction to counseling skills, advanced clinical skills, group counseling, intervention and treatment planning, psychopathology, and appraisal and assessment are some of the classes in which students learned core content, demonstrated competency in their academic work, and practiced the skills and techniques associated with the class. As we will discuss in the section on assessment, it is unlikely that students have reached fieldwork if they did not demonstrate capacity near the expectation level needed to move into fieldwork. With that acknowledgement, being at the expected level does not assume there is not ample work left to do to prepare interns to be career ready.

Practicum and internship texts highlight several clinical skills for faculty supervisors to teach and oversee, such as clinical writing, creating treatment plans, documenting case notes, crisis intervention, ending therapy (termination), building cultural competency, and guiding the overall counseling process (Hodges, 2024). Because CACREP (2024) does not require which standards are addressed in the fieldwork courses, programs and faculty have the freedom to determine which standards for clinical practice and knowledge are included in the course. The *Counselor Competencies Scale-Revised* is an evidence-based tool that assesses counseling skills and therapeutic conditions, and counseling dispositions and behaviors. The criterion in the assessment can be used as a guide for which skills faculty can focus on developing, monitoring, and assessing. The CCSR-R comprehensively covers professional behaviors and counseling skills that aid a counselor in being an effective counselor, but it does not specify which criterion students or interns need to be proficient in, above or beyond other ones, to be eligible for the degree and ready to practice.

It will not be the nature of this text to dictate which CACREP (2024) standards are more important than others and should be addressed in the fieldwork courses. *Section 2.C.c* and *d* of the standards dictates that key performance indicators must be assessed using multiple measures across multiple points in time, with a minimum of one KPI measured during fieldwork—but KPIs are not determined by CACREP, they are determined by programs. We can position ourselves to defend that basic counseling skills (Corey, 2019) are non-negotiable for the required proficiencies needed for counseling work post-degree. Many counseling programs will start with courses and utilize texts that begin with teaching basic counseling skills. Those courses typically fall in a sequence that starts with teaching basic skills before moving to advanced or specialized counseling skills.

That being said, it is possible that a student will reach the fieldwork phase without strong capacity in some basic skills and demonstrated capacity in specialized areas, such as group counseling or crisis intervention.

The potential paradoxes of disconnects between strengths in certain skills and deficiencies in others are endless. In the following chapter, we will discuss the imperative for ongoing assessment, and in this section, we raise awareness to the fact that a university supervisor will encounter a myriad of skill needs in students. While the commonly used texts give ideas for what to focus on, a faculty should not assume that they will not focus on basic skills addressed in previous classes, advanced skills that have not been covered or are being taught concurrently in other classes, or specialized topics that do not fall into the program sequence for learning.

To facilitate a systematic approach to prioritizing skill development for counseling interns, supervisors and faculty can employ a decision-making matrix. This matrix helps identify which skills require concentrated focus, based on common standards, client safety considerations, and professional readiness. This decision-making matrix can be adapted by programs or university supervisors, in addition to other evidence-based tools or scholarly texts (Table 3.1).

To use this matrix:

- Assess each intern's proficiency for each skill area at the outset and periodically during the internship. Determine which evidence-based tool will be used and how frequently.
- Factor in program requirements, site expectations, and client needs for the placement.
- Consider the potential impact of skill deficiencies on client safety and professional effectiveness.
- Assign an overall priority level for focused development, emphasizing high-priority areas that are foundational for safe, ethical, and effective practice.
- Adjust focus as the practicum and internship progress and as the intern demonstrates growth or identifies new needs.

This structured approach ensures that skill development is intentional, adaptive, and tailored to both program standards and the unique developmental trajectory of each counseling intern.

In addition to technical skills and structured assessments, the personal growth of interns should be viewed as a dynamic, longitudinal

TABLE 3.1 Decision-Making Matrix

Skill Area	Program Requirement	Intern's Demonstrated Proficiency	Client Safety/Risk	Professional Relevance	Immediate Fieldwork Needs	Priority Level
Basic Counseling Skills (e.g., active listening, empathy, rapport-building)	Required Core	Emerging/Proficient	High	Essential for all settings	Yes	High
Advanced Clinical Skills (e.g., assessment crisis intervention, treatment planning)	Varies by program	Developing	Moderate-High	Important for specialized settings	Depends on placement	Medium-High
Clinical Writing (e.g., case notes, documentation)	Required	Needs Improvement	Moderate	Essential	Yes	High
Emotional Maturity & Self-awareness	Implicit/Explicit	Varies	High (impacts client relationships)	Critical for professional growth	Always relevant	High
Professionalism	Required	Proficient/Needs Support	High	Universal relevance	Yes	High
Cultural Competency	Required/Best Practice	Emerging	Moderate-High	Essential for diverse clientele	Yes	High
Self-care	Best Practice	Varies	Indirect (impacts burnout/risk)	Critical for sustainability	Ongoing	Medium-High
Specialized Skill Areas (e.g., group counseling)	Electives/Placement-Dependent	Developing	Variable	Context-dependent	If applicable	Medium

process. As interns engage with clients and become more involved in the complexities of real-world practice, nuanced traits such as self-awareness, adaptability, and reflective capacity become increasingly important. Supervisors should encourage ongoing dialogue about not only skill acquisition but also the attitudes and personal qualities that influence client interactions and team collaboration. These qualities, while less tangible than discrete competencies, are foundational in shaping an intern's professional identity and ensuring the delivery of compassionate, ethical care. In sum, university supervisors are aware that skill development begins before fieldwork, is attended to deliberately through fieldwork, and is more than just clinical skills for the specialized area of counseling.

Emotional Maturity

Dispositions are a student's tendencies, state of mind, behaviors, and/or their outlooks. They are the visible and invisible forces that impact counseling work with clients, supervisors, peers, and other relevant constituents. The CACREP (2024) standards in *Section 1 M*.5 indicate that in counseling programs a student handbook is to be created and contain, "individual student assessment procedures, including key performance indicators and professional dispositions." Additionally in section 2, they indicate the following:

CACREP (2024) Section 2: Academic Quality

Individual Student Assessment: Standard C.2

2. *The counselor education program faculty systematically assess each student's professional dispositions throughout the program. The assessment process includes the following:*

   a. *identify and define professional dispositions to be assessed;*
   b. *measurement of student professional dispositions over multiple points in time; and*
   c. *review or analysis of individual student data for the purpose of retention, remediation, and dismissal.*

They do not provide a list of dispositions or emphasis on how to develop dispositions, but rather state in C.3, "The counselor education program has a systematic process in place for communicating feedback to students on their individual assessments of knowledge, skills, and professional dispositions."

The CCS-R provides 11 "Primary Professional Dispositions" that cover ethics, boundaries, behaviors, adherence to policies, emotional regulation, non-client clinical skills, cultural competency, and relevant cognitive tasks. In addition to the CCS-R, the American Counseling Association's *Code of Ethics* (2014) provides a comprehensive set of standards for clinical practice and professional behaviors that faculty and programs can consider when developing dispositions. Because the dispositions will be determined in advance, the focus of this section is understanding how dispositions, apart from clinical skills, impact readiness for the fieldwork phase and future counseling work. Additionally, there is a likelihood that a faculty supervisor will encounter emotional maturity issues and needs outside of the designated dispositions.

Dispositions for emotional maturity include an intern's capacity for self-reflection, emotional regulation, and resilience in the face of difficulty. Research highlights that the development of these dispositional traits is instrumental in preparing counselors for effective and ethical practice (Hill et al., 2021; Swank et al., 2022). Key aspects involve recognizing and naming one's own emotions, managing impulses, and demonstrating patience in stressful or uncertain situations. Emotionally mature interns can accept feedback constructively, respond rather than react under pressure, and sustain empathy and composure, even when confronted with challenging client dynamics (Moss et al., 2020). They model professional boundaries, possess a growth mindset, and demonstrate adaptability in their response—continually striving to align their actions with both ethical standards and personal values.

Supervisors play a pivotal role in fostering emotional maturity among counseling interns. The literature highlights the importance of modeling these dispositions—self-reflection, vulnerability, emotional regulation, and resilience—in supervisory relationships (Bernard & Goodyear, 2019). One key strategy identified is the consistent provision of constructive feedback within a supportive environment, helping interns process and integrate feedback rather than resist or dismiss it (Lambie et al., 2022). Supervisors also intentionally create opportunities for self-assessment, guiding interns to recognize and articulate their emotional responses during supervision and in their client work (Swank et al., 2022). Through reflective questions, open dialogue, and structured self-evaluation tools, they help interns develop awareness of their strengths, vulnerabilities, and growth areas.

Moreover, supervisors support interns through challenging situations by normalizing the experiences that students are having. They reinforce adaptive coping and encourage a growth mindset, helping interns reframe difficulties as opportunities for learning (Moss et al., 2020). In moments of stress or ethical uncertainty, supervisors model composure and ethical reasoning, inspiring interns to do the same. By prioritizing the cultivation of emotional maturity—through mentorship, feedback, and reflective practice—supervisors ensure that interns are not only clinically competent but also personally grounded, resilient, and ethically prepared for the demands of counseling.

When considering readiness for the field, current literature emphasizes ethical integrity and boundary maintenance as critical for ensuring interns act consistently with professional codes and program expectations (Robertson et al., 2022). In the chapters on assessment and legal and ethical issues, we go further into gatekeeping and remediation when students are deficient in dispositional areas. Table 3.2 is a checklist for university supervisors to consider as they conceptualize the work they will do when guiding the emotional development of interns.

TABLE 3.2 Emotional Maturity Checklist

Focus Area	Checklist Items
Self-reflection	Regularly assess and acknowledge your own feelings, behaviors, and motivations; Identify personal strengths and areas for improvement
Emotional Regulation	Effectively manage strong emotions in stressful or challenging situations; Demonstrate patience and impulse control with clients, peers, and supervisors
Resilience	Adapt constructively to setbacks, criticism, or client difficulties; Return to a baseline of calm after emotional or professional challenges
Constructive Feedback Acceptance	Receive and integrate feedback from supervisors and peers with openness; Use feedback as a tool for ongoing professional growth, not as personal criticism
Empathy and Composure	Maintain empathy and presence, even when confronted with client distress or conflict; Respond thoughtfully rather than react impulsively to high-stress situations
Professional Boundaries	Consistently uphold ethical and professional boundaries in all interactions; Recognize and address boundary challenges promptly and appropriately
Growth Mindset and Adaptability	Demonstrate a willingness to learn and adapt as new challenges or feedback arise; Reframe mistakes or setbacks as opportunities for learning and development
Alignment with Ethical Standards	Regularly reflect on whether actions and decisions align with ethical guidelines and personal values; Seek guidance when faced with ethical uncertainty or dilemmas

Professionalism

Outside of clinical skills, interns are also developing and enhancing professionalism skills essential for their future work. Empirical research discusses the importance of professionalism, including punctuality, preparedness, ethical conduct, respect, communication, and reliability, as foundational qualities for effective counselors (Borders et al., 2014; Bernard & Goodyear, 2019). Interpersonal effectiveness, which impacts work with clients and colleagues, is identified as a key competency in the supervision literature (Falender & Shafranske, 2007).

University supervisors play a pivotal role in cultivating these essential counseling and professionalism skills through supervision, teaching, and mentoring (Borders et al., 2014). While some professionalism skills may be assumed to be held by interns at the graduate level, evidence shows that direct attention to professional development is necessary, as academic success does not guarantee interpersonal effectiveness (Bernard & Goodyear, 2019; Johnson & Campbell, 2002). Specifically, in the digital era that interns are developing in, specific guidance on digital citizenship and professional online behaviors is needed. Certain behaviors, such as not using a cell phone during internship, may not be as obvious to interns as supervisors. Professional dress codes may be more ambiguous to interns than in previous generations of students. Supervisors must be attuned to and responsive to interns' needs for professionalism growth.

Creating an environment of trust and safety, where interns feel secure in sharing both strengths and challenges, is vital for effective supervision (Falender & Shafranske, 2007). When supervisors model openness to feedback, they demonstrate how constructive critique can foster professional growth (Bernard & Goodyear, 2019). Intentional strategies for addressing professionalism during fieldwork are recommended, including explicit discussion of topics such as professional dress, punctuality, attendance, crisis response, dual relationships, cell phone use, and ethical boundaries (Borders et al., 2014). The use of real-life scenarios and ethical codes, coupled with guided reflection, helps interns integrate ethical principles into practice (Johnson & Campbell, 2002). Additionally, university supervisors may adopt their own informed consent or contracts for use that detail the expected professional behaviors in class, on site, and in the communities in which interns reside. This may help prevent issues ahead of time, by not assuming interns will figure out all the expectations and providing the rules and boundaries for them to work within.

Supervisors are also encouraged to support a growth mindset and normalize the challenges interns encounter, which research links to increased adaptability and resilience (Dweck, 2006; Borders et al., 2014). By inviting authentic discussions and reframing challenges as opportunities, supervisors contribute to the reflective and adaptive capacities necessary for ethical, compassionate, and sustainable practice. Table 3.3 provides a guiding list of primary professional behaviors university supervisors can address or attend to during fieldwork. This list is not exhaustive and still contains an adequate breadth of topics.

TABLE 3.3 Essential Skills and Behaviors for Ethical and Effective Practice

Category	Key Practices
Ethical Conduct	Reflect on alignment with ethical guidelines and personal values; review and apply codes of ethics; seek supervision or consultation in ethical dilemmas
Respect and Communication	Demonstrate respect to clients, colleagues, supervisors, stakeholders; communicate clearly, professionally, compassionately; maintain confidentiality and boundaries; Come prepared with necessary materials and a clear agenda.
Reliability and Commitment	Fulfill responsibilities; follow through on commitments; notify relevant parties in absences or emergencies and provide reasons; Arrive on time for all sessions, meetings, and fieldwork commitments.
Professional Appearance and Conduct	Adhere to professional dress and decorum guidelines; use electronic devices appropriately in clinical and educational settings
Interpersonal Effectiveness	Engage respectfully and constructively; resolve conflicts professionally; seek guidance when needed
Growth Mindset and Adaptability	Willingness to learn and adapt; reframe mistakes as development opportunities; accept and incorporate feedback
Awareness of Professional Boundaries	Recognize and maintain boundaries; manage dual relationships and boundary dilemmas
Engagement in Supervision	Attend supervision regularly; come prepared to discuss cases; participate in feedback and goal-setting; model openness and vulnerability

Cultural Competence

Multicultural competence is an essential skill for effective counseling. Bernard and Goodyear (2019) posit that supervisors are accountable for attending to multicultural issues in supervision. The CACREP 2024 standards provide a section (Section 3: Foundational Counseling: B: Social and Cultural Identities and Experiences) for programs to address. Additionally, within the specialized practices, further emphasis is provided for areas of focus. The 2016 *Multicultural and Social Justice Counseling Competencies* developed by Ratts and colleagues provide an additional framework comprised of domains, attitudes, beliefs, knowledge, skills, and actions. This scholarly work is important for moving beyond knowledge standards into practice and action-based behaviors. The practicum and internship manuals, identified other chapters, also provide directions and ideas for supervisors (whether university level or site based) to follow. Therefore, the case has already been made that programs will focus on multicultural, social justice, and advocacy competency development.

We want to delineate between knowledge and skills. With counseling preparation programs providing a specific class on multicultural counseling, the knowledge-based standards are likely to be covered in advance, prior to fieldwork. Standards, needing to be addressed more than once, will have been covered in other classes as well. With fieldwork focusing on the practice of knowledge, university supervisors must consider how they foster the capacity to counsel cross-culturally. Therefore, there is a shift from competency into capacity, as students move from knowledge into skills.

Skills include, but are not limited to, case conceptualization with client demographics addressed with a multidimensional and intersectional viewpoint of culture, culturally responsive assessment and treatment planning, identifying advocacy opportunities for disenfranchised clients, social justice efforts in the surrounding community to dismantle barriers or agents that negatively impact mental health and access to services, and cross application of basic and advanced counseling skills. University supervisors can be proactive in determining areas of focus. They can build these areas of address into case study assignments and evaluations of skills shown in video recordings. They can also be responsive in their supervision work based on what interns bring into group supervision.

Cultural competence is addressed through structured activities that prompt self-examination of cultural identities and biases, exposure to diverse perspectives, and critical conversations about power, privilege, and social justice. These approaches are supported by the work of Ratts et al. (2016), who emphasize the importance of intentional skill-building and reflection in multicultural and social justice counseling competencies. Bernard and Goodyear (2019) further highlight that supervisors play a key role in facilitating these developmental opportunities within clinical supervision, ensuring that supervisees not only gain knowledge but also translate that knowledge into culturally responsive practice. Supervisors may assign readings, facilitate multicultural workshops, or invite guest speakers to deepen understanding and expand awareness.

Schauss and colleagues (2017) note that a barrier to the developmental work is the counselor in training's unwillingness to self-disclose in supervision. Thus, while a supervisor can employ a battery of quality training approaches, the emotional process required for self-examination is an entirely separate area to address. Additionally, a supervisor's ability to be culturally responsive in supervision (discussed in further chapters) does not assume that interns are developing in the competencies and capacities.

To break through the resistance, Schauss and colleagues (2017) suggest utilizing psychoanalytical approaches of free association and mindfulness to decrease the anxiety and fears that inhibit interns from sharing their experiences and struggles. University supervisors focus on strengthening the working alliance with interns to foster a setting in which interns will be willing to openly discuss and self-disclose. The goal of the free association work is to focus on the present moment, and the immediate thoughts and feelings interns have about the clients they are working with. The free association work can be fostered by the supervisor normalizing common experiences and issues, using their own self-disclosure, and showing empathy and compassion. Mindfulness is used in tandem ground the intern in the present moment and decreases anxiety and stress that arises.

Mindfulness, when used in supervision, can lead to a decrease in anxiety, increase coping abilities, and increase self-reported compassion (Shapiro et al., 2007; Campbell & Christopher, 2012). Additionally, mindfulness in supervision can foster greater empathy and compassion, enhance the therapeutic relationship, and increase self-efficacy in interns (Daniel et al., 2015). Readers will want to reference the model provided by Schauss and colleagues for further orientation with this approach. Through successful navigation and decreasing of the barriers that inhibit interns from engaging in multicultural competency and capacity development work, university supervisors can gain a pulse on the needs of interns and create a responsive plan for addressing the needs.

In the following section and Table 3.4, we provide guidance for university supervisors on approaches they can take as supervisors and with interns to foster cultural competency and capacity.

Strategies for Multicultural Competence and Capacity Development

Engagement in Supervision

- Attend supervision sessions regularly and punctually
- Prepare to discuss cases with cultural and social identity considerations
- Actively participate in feedback exchanges and goal-setting activities
- Model openness, vulnerability, and willingness to self-disclose

Cultural Competence Foundations

- Review and apply the CACREP 2024 Standards, Section 3, on Social and Cultural Identities and Experiences
- Familiarize oneself with 2016 Multicultural and Social Justice Counseling Competencies (Ratts et al.)
- Distinguish between knowledge-based standards and skill-based applications

Skill Development

- Practice case conceptualization with intersectional and multidimensional cultural perspectives
- Engage in culturally responsive assessment and treatment planning
- Identify advocacy opportunities for clients experiencing disenfranchisement
- Participate in social justice efforts within the local community to dismantle barriers to mental health
- Apply basic and advanced counseling skills across diverse cultural contexts

Structured Activities and Reflection

- Complete activities designed to prompt self-examination of cultural identities and biases

- Seek exposure to diverse perspectives through readings, workshops, and guest speakers
- Engage in critical conversations about power, privilege, and social justice
- Reflect regularly on personal growth in cultural competence and capacity

Overcoming Barriers to Self-disclosure

- Build strong working alliances with supervisors to create safe, open environments
- Participate in psychoanalytical approaches such as free association to reduce anxiety and fear of disclosure
- Engage in mindfulness practices to ground oneself in the present and manage stress
- Normalize common experiences and struggles through supervisor self-disclosure, empathy, and compassion

Mindfulness and Compassion in Supervision

- Incorporate mindfulness exercises into supervision sessions
- Monitor changes in anxiety, coping abilities, and self-reported compassion
- Foster empathy and compassion to enhance therapeutic relationships and increase self-efficacy
- Reference existing models such as Schauss et al. (2017) for integrating mindfulness and free association

Continuous Assessment and Responsive Planning

- Evaluate multicultural skills through case study assignments and video-recorded sessions
- Adapt supervision approaches based on interns' needs and presenting issues
- Maintain a pulse on emerging barriers and create targeted plans to address them.

Table 3.4 provides guidance on foundational categories of cultural competency along with activities and focus areas for supervisors to integrate into their work.

TABLE 3.4 Cultural Competency Development

Category	Key Activities/ Standards	Focus Areas
Engagement in Supervision	Prepare, participate, and model openness	Discuss cases with cultural context; engage in feedback; demonstrate vulnerability
Cultural Competence Foundations	Study standards and competencies	Apply CACREP (2024) Standards; review Multicultural and Social Justice Counseling Competencies; understand key domains and distinctions
Skill Development	Practice and apply culturally responsive skills	Case conceptualization; assessment; advocacy; social justice; counseling across cultures
Structured Activities and Reflection	Self-examination and exposure	Reflect on identity and bias; seek diverse perspectives; engage in critical dialogue; monitor growth
Overcoming Barriers to Self-disclosure	Foster safe, open environments	Build alliances; use psychoanalytical and mindfulness approaches; normalize struggles
Mindfulness and Compassion in Supervision	Integrate mindfulness and empathy	Use exercises in supervision; monitor change; reference models; promote compassion
Continuous Assessment and Planning	Evaluate and adapt approaches	Assess multicultural skills; tailor supervision; address barriers as they arise

Conclusion

In this chapter, we break down the areas of development that university supervisors are responsible for attending to, teaching, cultivating, and enhancing. One may view them as indivisible from each other. To execute the necessary counseling skills, emotional maturity is vital when interns are navigating difficult clients, groups, and work-place factors. In that navigation, professionalism is foundational and a compass for working through the challenges. Cultural competence and capacity extend into the foundation, skills, and behaviors and give directions for the work being done immediately and broadly. In short, a university supervisor has a big responsibility for preparing interns to be comprehensively ready for the specialized field they are entering into.

References

Bernard, J. M., & Goodyear, R. K. (2019). *Fundamentals of clinical supervision* (6th ed.). Upper Saddle River, NJ: Pearson Education.

Borders, L. D. et al. (2014). Best practices in clinical supervision: Evolution of a counseling specialty. *The Clinical Supervisor, 33*(1), 26–44.

Campbell, J. C., & Christopher, J. C. (2012). Teaching mindfulness to create effective counselors. *Journal of Mental Health Counseling, 34*(3), 213–226.

Corey, G. (2019). *The art of integrative counseling.* Alexandria, VA: American Counseling Association.

Council for Accreditation of Counseling and Related Educational Programs (CACREP). (2024). *2024 Standards.* Retrieved from https://www.cacrep.org/for-programs/2024-cacrep-standards/

Daniel, L., Borders, L. D., & Willse, J. (2015). The role of supervisors' and supervisees' mindfulness in clinical supervision. *Counselor Education & Supervision, 54*(3), 221–232.

Dweck, C. S. (2006). *Mindset: The new psychology of success.* New York, NY: Random House.

Falender, C. A., & Shafranske, E. P. (2007). Competence in competency-based supervision practice: Construct and application. *Professional Psychology: Research and Practice, 38*(3), 232–240.

Hill, C. E., Sullivan, C., Knox, S., & Schlosser, L. Z. (2021). *Becoming a therapist: On the path to mastery.* Washington, DC: American Psychological Association.

Hodges, S. (2024). *The counseling practicum and internship manual: A resource for graduate counseling students in a dynamic global era* (4th ed.). New York, NY: Springer.

Johnson, E. J., & Campbell, J. M. (2002). Character and fitness requirements for professional counselors: Ethics, evaluation, and remediation. *Counselor Education and Supervision, 41*(3), 199–210.

Lambie, G. W., Blount, A. J., & Mullen, P. R. (2022). *Counseling supervision: Principles, process, and practice.* Alexandria, VA: American Counseling Association.

Moss, D., Gibson, D. M., & Dollarhide, C. T. (2020). Professional disposition development in counseling trainees: A review of the literature. *Journal of Counseling & Development, 98*(3), 277–286.

Ratts, M. J., Singh, A. A., Nassar-McMillan, S., Butler, S. K., & McCullough, J. R. (2016). Multicultural and social justice counseling competencies: Guidelines for the counseling profession. *Journal of Multicultural Counseling & Development, 44*(1), 28–48.

Robertson, D. L., Zaklak, J., & Meany-Walen, K. K. (2022). Navigating ethical boundaries in counseling supervision. *Counselor Education and Supervision, 61*(4), 301–316.

Schauss, E., Steinruck, R. E., & Brown, M. H. (2017). Mindfulness and free association for multicultural competence: A model for clinical group supervision. *Journal of Counselor Practice, 8*(2), 102–119.

Shapiro, S. L., Brown, K. W., & Biegel, G. M. (2007). Teaching self-care to caregivers: Effects of mindfulness-based stress reduction on the mental health of therapists in training. *Training and Education in Professional Psychology, 1*(2), 105–115.

Swank, J. M., Smith-Adcock, S., & Leggett, E. S. (2022). Counselor self-awareness: A review and future directions. *Journal of Counseling & Development, 100*(2), 123–133.

CHAPTER 4

ASSESSMENT

Abstract

Assessment and evaluation are pillars of a standards-driven counseling program. Practice of these behaviors is continuous, deliberate, and intentional for each stage in the developmental learning process. University supervisors evaluate the essential dimensions, as discussed in previous chapters, of the fieldwork phase. That includes competence, personal and professional growth, and career readiness. The assessment process is layered with objective standards, evidence-based criteria, and subjective insights. There will be systematic approaches for all interns as well as responsive approaches for the unique needs of each intern. In this chapter, we discuss the role of the university supervisor in assessing interns, methods for assessment, and essential tasks of assessment.

Role of Assessment

Much of the system for assessment is determined in advance as a part of the larger CACREP (2024) standards approach. As we have mentioned, assessment should be a continuous process throughout the course of a counseling program, whether master's or doctoral level (Briggs & Miller, 2005; Bernard & Goodyear, 2019). With the global context of assessment areas, university supervisors must operate in a designed process that allows continuous feedback, opportunities to intervene, and the ability to support growth. Assessment, in this chapter's regard, is beyond the grading of assignments and is more globally focused. Assessment in the context of university supervision will ensure that interns have acquired the necessary skills for their future professional identity, can adhere to ethical standards, that there is no foreseeable threat to do harm to clients,

DOI: 10.4324/9781003356776-5

can behave in a professional manner in all systems of their future career setting, and are "ready" to enter the career field.

Assessment needs to be a clearly identified process for both university supervisors and interns. There need to be pre-determined timelines-typically at the beginning, middle, and end of fieldwork. There needs to be pre-selected methods and measures. Ideally, the tools and measures used for assessment should have been introduced and practiced in earlier coursework, so that the practicum and internship do not serve as the first exposure to these evaluation methods. Additionally, the chosen measures will have been utilized in previous courses and will not be utilized for the first time in practicum and internship. Counseling programs identify assessment points, and university supervisors may dictate when additional assessment points occur throughout the term. The process should not be decided upon in the middle of the academic term, nor in a reactionary method.

While programs create key performance indicators, disposition, program, and student learning outcomes that are globally based and not inherently tied to CACREP (2024) standards, we encourage using evidence-based assessments to avoid subjective and biased behaviors that lead to inaccurate evaluations and inhibit growth and success of interns (Bernard & Goodyear, 2019; Briggs & Miller, 2005). We acknowledge that programs may, and often, develop their own rubrics to assess various types of standards. Research emphasizes that objective, validated assessment tools contribute to more reliable and equitable evaluations in counselor education (Swank & Lambie, 2016; Borders et al., 2014). Lastly, the assessment process must be inclusive of specific directions for university supervisors when interns are deficient. That includes communication with the fieldwork coordinator, department chairs or program directors, site supervisors and the intern. It will also include directions for supporting growth and/or the use of remediation plans (Bhat, 2019; Henderson & Dufrene, 2018).

Methods of Assessment

Assessment approaches can be formative and summative. Formative assessments are the ongoing evaluations aimed to provide constructive feedback and promote learning throughout the fieldwork phase. They can be driven by evidence-based tools, program developed rubrics, or live-feedback, or combination of the three. Summative assessments are comprehensive evaluations at designated times (beginning, middle, and end) of the fieldwork phase to determine the overall competence and readiness for independent practice. Below, we expand on the variety of assessment methods for formative and summative assessment.

Formative Approaches

When using electronic means, university supervisors work to maintain confidentiality, privacy, and compliance with legal and ethical statutes.

Direct Observation: observation of counseling (master's level), teaching, or supervision (doctoral level) in real time or via recordings. This allows for assessment of skills, attitudes, and professional behaviors. Ideally, rubrics or evidence measures will also be associated with the observation assessment to provide interns with advanced awareness of the objective criteria being observed and to legitimize the feedback away from subjective bias.

Self-assessment: approaches encourage interns to reflect holistically on their growth and development. These approaches can include journaling, online discussion forums, peer support groups, or creative and reflective exercises in and outside of the course. The university supervisors carefully consider how to engage, so as not to interfere with the authentic and vulnerable process. They pay attention to emerging themes and trends that qualitatively emerge and decide how to proceed with support.

Client Feedback: in tandem with the site supervisor, prescriptive measures can be utilized to gain client feedback and thusly assess intern effectiveness. For doctoral students this could include classroom feedback from teaching, supervisee feedback from supervision, or clients in clinical settings. University supervisors determine a schedule in advance for collecting this information and when to discuss with the intern.

Site Supervisor Evaluations: site supervisors evaluate their interns in both formative and summative methods. Formative evaluations include ongoing communication from check-ins (email, phone calls, live visits). We encourage the use of rubrics and other measures, such as progress sheets, when engaging in formative assessments with supervisors. The measures should be pre-determined in order that site supervisors are aware of their expectations and interns are aware of how they are being evaluated in measure and frequency. Evidence-based tools can be used as well as program developed rubrics. Whichever measure is used; it should be clear, concise, and efficient for use to minimize time and confusion.

Peer Feedback: peer feedback is a component of several group supervision approaches. University supervisors will attend to the emerging themes and qualitative insights of peers to determine the next steps involved in supporting intern's growth. Rubrics can be helpful for peers to have a focus on areas of feedback to provide. Additionally, the organic and free association process is also encouraged.

Case Presentations: this approach differs from live observation in that a recording or demonstration is not required. Case presentations can be structured assignments or in-class activities. This allows interns to display competencies for case conceptualization, treatment planning, intervention planning, social justice and advocacy, systems work, and a variety of relevant areas related to the professional identity of the interns. We recommend using rubrics that designate the competencies to be evaluated so that interns are aware of the focus of the work and how they are being assessed. These approaches can be imbedded in the prescribed learning sequence or responsive if university supervisors deem that further development in this area is needed.

Review of Documentation: this approach provides university supervisors with the ability to assess interns' documentation that can include case notes, treatment plans, classroom lessons, program planning, group plans, or other relevant materials for the professional identity of the interns. This should be a prescribed approach via an assignment and done collaboratively with the site supervisor. Additionally, we encourage the use of rubrics for evaluation.

Rubrics: Research identifies several best practices for developing effective rubrics in educational and supervisory settings. Rubrics should be directly aligned with learning objectives and desired outcomes, ensuring clarity and transparency in assessment (Stevens & Levi, 2013; Brookhart, 2018). Criteria and performance levels must be clearly described to distinguish levels of achievement and reduce ambiguity (Andrade, 2005). Involving key stakeholders—including faculty, supervisors, and students—in the development process enhances both validity and cultural relevance (Jonsson & Svingby, 2007). Pilot testing and iterative revision help identify unclear items and improve reliability (Popham, 1997). Integrating both qualitative and quantitative criteria supports a more holistic evaluation (Jonsson & Svingby, 2007). Finally, clear guidance and training on rubric use are essential for consistent and fair scoring (Brookhart, 2018).

Summative Approaches

Competency Measures: programs determine in advance when evidence-based measures are used for evaluation. In this book, we have espoused the Counseling Competencies Scale-Revised (CCS-R). As mentioned, its use should occur before the fieldwork phase and can be used to determine if students are ready for internship. Mid-term evaluations and end-of-term evaluations are relevant points in time for utilization. University supervisors and site supervisors can complete this evaluation for assessment.

Site visits: site visits are not a CACREP (2024) required practice but are common across counseling preparation programs. Site visits can be pre-determined, outside of regular communication with supervisors, and inclusive of a summative assessment. A site visit midterm can include a competency measure to assess progress and identify areas of growth for focus. As site supervisors complete an evaluation measure at the end of the academic term, university supervisors and site supervisors can compare progress from mid-term to end of term. Early in fieldwork, such as in practicum, this practice can be helpful for determining readiness to move on in fieldwork.

Table 4.1 provides a decision-making guide for selecting assessment types based on intern developmental stage, goals, and context.

TABLE 4.1 Assessment Choice Guide

Assessment Type	When to Use	Key Considerations
Formative Assessment	Throughout internship, especially early and mid-stage	– Monitor ongoing development – Provide feedback for growth – Use for setting and adjusting goals
Summative Assessment	End of internship or major learning phase	– Evaluate overall achievement – Determine readiness for next stage – Meet institutional/legal requirements
Self-assessment	Regular intervals; goal-setting sessions	– Encourage personal reflection – Promote ownership of growth – Foster self-directed learning
Peer Assessment	Group activities, collaborative projects	– Gain multiple perspectives – Support social development – Build teamwork skills
Supervisor Observation	Ongoing, especially during fieldwork	– Assess real-time performance – Address qualitative factors – Ensure holistic and cultural sensitivity
Standardized Assessment	When objective benchmarking is needed	– Compare to norms – Fulfill program or licensure needs – Use with caution for cross-cultural relevance

We encourage programs to combine multiple approaches for a comprehensive evaluation, and to consider holistic, cultural, and legal factors throughout the process.

Feedback

Feedback is a vital tool in advancing intern development and overall assessment efficacy. Feedback that is timely, specific, balanced, collaborative, and action-oriented is consistently associated with improved intern performance and professional growth (Major & Ward, 2023). Supervisors often face challenges due to the emotional intensity and sensitivity inherent in delivering feedback, particularly when remediation is required (Hoffman et al., 2022). The tendency to avoid difficult conversations can compromise both learning outcomes and self-efficacy for interns (Bernard & Goodyear, 2019).

Contemporary studies highlight that creating a psychologically safe environment—where feedback is viewed as an opportunity for growth, not criticism—is foundational for effective supervision (Fouad et al., 2021). Both interns and supervisors benefit from adopting a growth mindset and engaging in reflective practices that foster open dialogue and constructive feedback (Moss, 2020). Interns are encouraged to demonstrate professional behaviors when receiving feedback, while existing literature also emphasizes that supervisors should consider their methods to deliver feedback in ways that support growth and reduce potential negative effects.

To avoid being punitive or harsh when giving feedback, supervisors should foster a supportive environment rooted in a strong supervisory alliance with the intern (Bernard & Goodyear, 2019). The alliance should embody empathy and be collaborative, as research consistently shows that a strong supervisory relationship is associated with intern satisfaction and professional growth (Fouad et al., 2021; Moss, 2020). Feedback is most constructive when it is specific, balanced, and framed as an opportunity for development rather than as a critique of character or capability (Major & Ward, 2023). Supervisors can focus on observable behaviors, use nonjudgmental language, and highlight strengths alongside areas for improvement (Hoffman et al., 2022). Outlining the feedback process in advance allows interns to anticipate next steps and promotes teamwork, as indicated by Fouad et al., (2021).

When supervisors approach feedback as a partnership, emphasizing respect and ongoing dialogue, the process becomes an empowering catalyst for learning instead of a punitive exercise. Supervisors will benefit from utilizing mindfulness practices to become self-aware of the experiences with supervisors in their professional journey that have shaped their understanding of the supervisor's relationship—whether good or bad. This work will allow supervisors to increase practices that empower interns and decrease mindless practices that decrease self-efficacy and cause harm. Table 4.2 provides a self-reflection guidance chart for university supervisors to consider in their assessment and feedback work.

TABLE 4.2 Guiding Self-awareness and Growth in the Feedback Process

Reflection Question

Have I clearly communicated the process to the intern so they know what to expect and how they are involved?

Am I approaching this feedback session from a place of empathy and partnership, rather than authority or critique?

How can I ensure my feedback is specific, actionable, and balanced—highlighting both strengths and areas for growth?

In what ways do my own professional experiences with feedback influence how I deliver it now? Are there practices I want to emulate or avoid?

Have I taken time to be mindful and self-aware of my emotional state before engaging in this feedback conversation?

Am I using nonjudgmental language that focuses on observable behaviors, rather than personal traits or character?

How can I foster a supportive environment that encourages a growth mindset in the intern?

Have I checked in with the intern about their comfort level and readiness to receive feedback?

Do I balance constructive criticism with genuine acknowledgment of the intern's strengths and progress?

In what ways am I open to ongoing dialogue and collaborative action planning with the intern, rather than viewing feedback as a one-way process?

How can I ensure my feedback empowers the intern and builds their self-efficacy, rather than diminishing their confidence?

Are there mindful practices—such as taking a pause to reflect, deep breathing, or recalling positive supervision experiences—that I can use to center myself before and during the feedback process?

Am I aware of any tendencies to avoid difficult feedback, and how can I address these tendencies to ensure the intern receives the feedback they need for growth?

Developmental Concerns

Assessment needs to be conscious of developmental stages, taking into account where interns are positioned within their learning trajectory. In practicum, when interns are in the beginning stages of fieldwork, they often require greater scaffolding, direct observation, and frequent formative feedback (Borders, 2021; Bernard & Goodyear, 2019). Intermediate interns, approaching the end of practicum or progressing through internship courses, typically demonstrate increased autonomy and self-efficacy. These individuals benefit from collaborative engagement and assignments that build advanced clinical, supervisory, or teaching skills (Stoltenberg & McNeill, 2010). Advanced interns, nearing the completion of their fieldwork, are often ready to exhibit independent practice, leadership, and the integration of complex theories and concepts into their counseling work.

Supervisors need to be mindful that while we expect interns to advance through the developmental stages in progression, interns do not uniformly begin at the same stage, nor do they progress at the same rate. As well, some interns will not move beyond the intermediate stage but may still be ready for their future professional work. Because the assessments themselves do not evolve with the interns, supervisors are cognizant that scores, for example, on a 1–5 scale, may be around 3 or even 2 in the beginning stages. Reasonably, supervisors will expect scores to reach a minimum of 3 during the intermediate phase. Reaching a 4 or 5 during advanced stages is also a reasonable expectation. Given the subjective nature of rating scales and lack of evolution of the scales used across the fieldwork phase, we encourage university supervisors, site supervisors, and coordinators or other relevant department personnel to collaborate toward reaching a shared understanding and unified approach when using any assessment tool or method.

Ethical Considerations

Assessment exerts a profound influence on a student's educational and career trajectory (Borders, 2021; Bernard & Goodyear, 2019). Supervisors are called to uphold fairness, transparency, and cultural sensitivity at every stage. Utilizing systematic assessment instruments and rubrics—recognized best practice in counselor education (Stoltenberg & McNeill, 2010)—university supervisors must also engage in qualitative reflection, attending to holistic factors that shape intern development. Research in counseling encourages consideration of developmental variables such as age, lived experience, learning styles, ability, systemic influences, and cross-cultural dimensions (Bernard & Goodyear, 2019; Borders, 2021). Instruments must be critically evaluated for cultural relevance and carefully interpreted through a human development lens (Stoltenberg & McNeill, 2010; Bernard & Goodyear, 2019). An example is having proficiency in the use of technology. Questions a supervisor can consider are: what exposure has the individual had to technology? What technology has been available during their lifespan? What, if any, cross-cultural considerations are there? There are just a few questions to consider for just one example. University supervisors must maintain a pulse on the demographics, systemic influences, and holistic factors affecting their students' development to identify subsequent areas to question.

As supervisors work collaboratively with counseling departments or embark on their own for choosing and developing assessment methods, we provide a beginning guiding checklist for consideration that addresses ethical and cultural considerations (see Table 4.3). In subsequent chapters, we discuss culturally responsive supervision, coordination practices, remediation, and ethical/legal concerns. Briefly, we note that digital platforms are the commonly used approach for completing, disseminating, and storing assessment documents. Departments will consider the best practices for confidentiality and security for storing records.

TABLE 4.3 Assessment Considerations

Checklist Item	Description
Use unbiased assessment tools	Ensure assessment methods and instruments are free from bias.
Recognize cultural assumptions	Be aware of personal cultural views and their impact on assessment.
Accommodate diverse backgrounds	Support interns' varied backgrounds and learning styles.
Maintain confidentiality	Keep assessment data private, sharing only with authorized personnel.
Maintain records for legal/ academic use	Keep all records as required by institutional and legal guidelines.
Assess developmental stage	Evaluate interns according to their current stage of human growth and learning.
Encourage personal growth	Support interns in setting and achieving goals that foster their overall development.
Consider holistic factors	Take into account physical, emotional, cognitive, and social aspects that influence development.

Conclusion

Assessment is a nuanced and complex process comprised of both qualitative and quantitative factors. There are multiple approaches a supervisor can take, and we strongly encourage that assessment is woven through the entire learning and development sequence, not solely in fieldwork. Assessment approaches need to be intentional and relevant for the developmental stage interns are in. They need to be cross-culturally relevant and sensitive to holistic factors that influence interns' progression. Inevitably, when using one-size-fits-all approaches with pre-formatted assessments, supervisors will run into situations where the qualitative factors are very significant and need to be analyzed thoroughly. Therefore, supervisors must maintain appropriate levels of cultural competency and actively infuse cultural sensitivity in their assessment work. The goal of assessment is to not only determine acquisition of learning content and stage of development for performance, but also foster growth and success. Supervisors continuously reflect on their approaches, bracket biases, and address their own barriers to fair and equitable assessment.

References

Andrade, H. L. (2005). Teaching with rubrics: The good, the bad, and the ugly. *College Teaching, 53*(1), 27–31.

Bernard, J. M., & Goodyear, R. K. (2019). *Fundamentals of clinical supervision.* Upper Saddle River, NJ: Pearson.

Bhat, C. S. (2019). Remediation plans in counselor education. *Journal of Counselor Preparation and Supervision, 12,* 1–16.

Borders, L. D. (2021). Best practices in clinical supervision: Evolution and current status. *Clinical Supervisor, 40*(1), 1–22.

Borders, L. D., Glosoff, H. L., Welfare, L. E., Hays, D. G., DeKruyf, L., Fernando, D. M., & Page, B. (2014). Best practices in clinical supervision: Evolution of a counseling specialty. *The Clinical Supervisor, 33*(1), 44–63.

Briggs, M., & Miller, G. (2005). *Assessment in counselor education.* Alexandris, VA: American Counseling Association.

Brookhart, S. M. (2018). *How to create and use rubrics for formative assessment and grading.* Alexandria, VA: ASCD.

Council for Accreditation of Counseling and Related Educational Programs (CACREP). (2024). *2024 Standards.* Retrieved from https://www.cacrep.org/for-programs/2024-cacrep-standards/

Fouad, N. A., et al. (2021). Competency benchmarks: A model for understanding and measuring competence in professional psychology. *Training and Education in Professional Psychology, 15*(2), 79–90.

Henderson, K., & Dufrene, R. (2018). Supervision and remediation in counselor training. *Counselor Education and Supervision, 57*(3), 163–177.

Hoffman, R., et al. (2022). Supervisory feedback practices and supervisee outcomes: A systematic review. *Journal of Counseling Psychology, 69*(4), 411–427.

Jonsson, A., & Svingby, G. (2007). The use of scoring rubrics: Reliability, validity and educational consequences. *Educational Research Review, 2*(2), 130–144.

Major, J., & Ward, L. (2023). Creating effective feedback in clinical supervision: Strategies and pitfalls. *Clinical Supervisor, 42*(1), 24–37.

Moss, D. (2020). Growth mindset in supervision: Fostering intern resilience and learning. *Counselor Education and Supervision, 59*(3), 191–205.

Popham, W. J. (1997). What's wrong—and what's right—with rubrics. *Educational Leadership, 55*(2), 72–75.

Stevens, D. D., & Levi, A. J. (2013). *Introduction to rubrics: An assessment tool to save grading time, convey effective feedback, and promote student learning* (2nd ed.). Sterling, VA: Stylus Publishing.

Stoltenberg, C. D., & McNeill, B. W. (2010). *Counselor development and supervision theory: The integrated developmental model.* Oxfordshire: Routledge.

Swank, J. M., & Lambie, G. W. (2016). Evaluating assessment tools in counselor education. *Measurement and Evaluation in Counseling and Development, 49*(4), 267–279.

CHAPTER 5

COORDINATING FIELDWORK PROGRAMS

Abstract

Coordinating fieldwork programs is complex and equally as challenging as teaching university supervision courses. Programs are not obligated to appoint a separate fieldwork coordinator but having one is an available option. Accreditation standards (CACREP, 2024) provide foundational guidance for programs to build off, and a coordinator will be hard pressed to find many or even a few more resources to guide the coordination work. We recognize the value of creatively interpreting standards for each program, while also highlighting the complex coordinator role in ensuring accreditation compliance. Therefore, the purpose of this chapter is to bring visibility to the layers involved in coordination work as coordinators strive to adhere to accreditation standards.

Designing Fieldwork Experiences

Effective programming begins with an intentional design. The fieldwork framework must contain relevant accreditation standards, program standards, and dispositions that will be a foundation for faculty, doctoral students who supervise during internship, and master's and doctoral-level interns. Essentially, the fieldwork objectives need to align with accreditation and desired program outcomes. That design work should be done collaboratively with faculty, program stakeholders and advisor committees, site supervisors, and even students.

This design work is continuous and evolves with changes in accreditation standards, program needs, and student needs. Coordinators will determine, based on both accreditation tenants and author suggested items:

- When students can begin fieldwork
- Placing or providing resources for placements
- How many sections of practicum and internship are needed each semester
- How many cycles of internship students take
- The day and time of the course
- Schedule of site visits
- Assessment and evaluation methods and schedules
- Use of technology platforms for record keeping
- Evaluations methods for students to evaluate site supervisors and sites
- Site supervisor orientation methods
- Ongoing training for site supervisors
- Gate keeping and remediation methods
- Whether or not students participate in readiness programming prior to fieldwork
- Supervision for university supervisors

This list, while robust for the array of responsibilities, is not all inclusive. The list is a helpful starting point, and many of us learn as we go along each academic year. As we mentioned, coordinators are continuously monitoring all the elements of fieldwork and will need to be flexible and adaptable to make necessary changes.

Fieldwork Handbook

Whether starting from scratch or stepping into the coordinator role with a provided framework or materials, a starting point can be with developing or revising the handbook or manual. A fieldwork handbook, also known as the practicum and internship manual, is required by accreditation standards. CACREP (2024) standard G in the *Practice* section details what the manual is required to contain. It provides required sections but does not provide subsequent details as to what each section needs to expand upon. This allows freedom for each program to determine what is relevant for their program, students, and potential sites. A handbook is a legal document in its own way as it provides informed consent for all relevant parties on expectations, requirements, and policies. We argue that more is more in the case of creating a handbook.

Required (CACREP, 2024) elements include:

- Handbook must be available to all students, site supervisors and for all program delivery types
- Provide detailed requirements
- Detail expectations, policies, and procedures
- Contain accreditation standards and definitions related to supervised fieldwork
- Supervision agreement
- Evaluation procedures and requirements
- Policies for retention, remediation, and dismissal

Suggested elements by the author, include:

- Securing sites and placement timelines
- Information on required amount and types of fieldwork hours
- Legal and ethical considerations
- Remediation plans
- Removal from a site or fieldwork
- How to search for sites or switching sites mid-term
- Criteria for program approved sites
- Student employment at internship sites
- Boundaries for settings of clinical work
- Required experiences at site
- Interning at multiple sites
- Expectations for approved supervisors
- Illness and absences
- Requesting new sites or changing sites
- Self-care and wellness
- Liability insurance requirements (required by accreditation)

While there may be more areas than listed to consider coordinators must determine how to orient interns and site supervisors with the handbook. Additionally, we strongly encourage a consent form embedded in the handbook that interns and supervisors sign, affirming they understand the expectations and requirements. Several methods for orientation are possible: fieldwork bootcamp, organized in-person meeting, virtual pre-recorded training, online modules for specific sections. Whichever the approach is, orienting individuals with the handbook is equally as important as having a robust manual.

Course Sequence

With 60 credits required by CACREP (2024) for master's level programs, program sequence length is commonly two to three years, with exceptions in between depending on circumstances. Doctoral sequences will vary based on dissertation and relevant program factors. Therefore, we focus on master's level sequences to provide examples. Possible sequences, developed by the author with some considerations for accreditation standards, for master's level fieldwork are bulleted below, with each bullet point from practicum respectively referencing the internship bullet point:

- Two-year program:
  - Practicum
    - Practicum begins second semester of year one
    - Practicum begins summer term of year one
    - Practicum begins first semester of year two
  - Internship
    - Internship begins summer term of year one
      - Two to three courses for internship, year or more long, part time internship
    - Internship begins first semester of year two
      - Two courses, year-long, part time internship
    - Internship begins second semester of year two
      - One course, one semester, full time internship
- Three-year program:
  - Practicum
    - Practicum begins second semester of year two
    - Practicum begins summer semester of year two
  - Internship
    - Internship begins summer semester of year two
      - Two to three courses for internship, year or more long, part time

- Internship begins first semester of year three
  - Two courses for internship, yearlong, part time

While accreditation does not require how many internship courses need to be offered, there are set hour requirements. Practicum students must complete a minimum of 100 hours over a full academic term that is a minimum of eight weeks consistent with the academic calendar (CACREP, 2024, 4.Q). Forty of those hours must be direct. Internship students must complete 600 hours in their specialized practice area with 240 hours being direct hours with actual clients (CACREP, 2024, 4. U, V). With that understanding, we encourage coordinators to reflect on the development learning sequence prior to and concurrent with fieldwork. Additionally, we encourage critically thinking about what is in the student's best interest for the required length of fieldwork, as it pertains to the specialized practice.

For example, a full-time internship over the course of a 15-week term will require around 40 hours of work per week. A minimum of 16 of those 40 hours will need to be direct client contact. This will be in addition to anywhere from one to three academic courses that demand anywhere from three to six hours each for classroom and academic work time. A school counseling intern may benefit from a full-time internship as it allows for deeper immersion into the intricate school systems and allows them to see a full school semester from start to finish. Clients are more immediately available and completing the group work standard is more feasible. For clinical mental health interns, this may not be appropriate given the varied nature of clinical work with cancellations, no-shows, client-turn over, and lack of control in attrition. A one semester full-time design for internship may set students up for failure.

It is important to note that hours should not be the sole dictator for sequence design. The hour requirements are a starting point, and programs may choose to add more hours for their requirements. Requiring a full-time internship may be deemed as the best practice for the developmental learning needs regardless of the hour requirements.

The workload demands of academic courses in addition to fieldwork need to be considered. It may be less realistic to plan for fieldwork after the completion of all knowledge courses due to the likelihood of extending program completion time. Therefore, the likelihood that students are taking academic courses whilst in fieldwork is high. Fundamental courses that can be completed prior to fieldwork include introductory courses, basic and advanced skills, crisis intervention, theories, multicultural counseling, crisis intervention, assessment, research, teaching, and relevant introductory specialty courses for professional identity.

Courses to be taken concurrently can include group counseling, advanced specialty courses, capstone, treatment planning, practice-inspired standard-based coursework. We would be ill conceived to prescribe one approach. Rather, we reflect that program chairs, fieldwork coordinators, and department faculty reflect critically on the minimum required knowledge to begin practicing in fieldwork as they determine program course sequences.

Assessment Schedule and Selection of Assessments

Assessment is a continuous process throughout the fieldwork experience. As we have mentioned in other chapters, it should begin before the fieldwork phase. Determining readiness for fieldwork is an essential effort in gate-keeping practices. We will provide specific ideas for assessment schedules and assessment instruments utilizing the same possible course sequences mentioned above. Coordinators must remember that assessment is not solely for advancing through the program sequence but also for advancing to enter the counseling field in each respective professional identity. The critical nature of assessment increases in intensity as the intern gets closer to completing the program. Therefore, especially when using pre-formatted instruments systematically, whomever is evaluating takes into account where interns are at developmentally, what is needed at that phase in fieldwork, and the minimum requirements to move onto the next phase in sequence. A hypothetical sequence, developed by the author with some considerations for accreditation standards, is provided below.

- Two-year program:
  - Practicum
    - Practicum begins second semester of year one
      - *Assess readiness in skills courses*
      - *Determine advancement to fieldwork in between first and second semester*
      - *Assess midterm and end of term in practicum*
      - *Determine internship readiness after practicum term*

- Practicum begins summer term of year one

  - *Assess readiness in skills courses and relevant professional identity courses*
  - *Determine advancement to fieldwork after second semester*
  - *Assess midterm and end of term in practicum*
  - *Determine internship readiness after practicum term*

- Practicum begins first semester of year two

  - *Assess readiness in skills courses and relevant professional identity courses*
  - *Determine advancement to fieldwork after full academic term*
  - *Assess midterm and end of term in practicum*
  - *Determine internship readiness after practicum term*

- Internship

  - Internship begins summer term of year one

    - Two to three courses for internship, year or more long, part time internship

      - *Assess progress mid-term and end of term*
      - *Determine readiness for second or third course at completion of each term*

  - Internship begins first semester of year two

    - Two courses, year-long, part time internship

      - *Assess progress mid-term and end of term*
      - *Determine readiness for second course at completion of each term*

  - Internship begins second semester of year two

    - One course, one semester, full time internship

      - *Assess progress mid-term and end of term*

- Three-year program:

  - Practicum

    - Practicum begins second semester of year two

      - *Assess readiness in skills courses and relevant professional identity courses*
      - *Determine advancement to fieldwork after first academic year and second term in second year*

- *Assess midterm and end of term in practicum*
- *Determine internship readiness after practicum term*
- Practicum begins summer semester of year two
  - *Assess readiness in skills courses and relevant professional identity courses*
  - *Determine advancement to fieldwork after first academic year and second academic year*
  - *Assess midterm and end of term in practicum*
  - *Determine internship readiness after practicum term*
- Internship
  - Internship begins summer semester of year two
    - Two to three courses for internship, year or more long, part time
      - *Assess progress mid-term and end of term*
      - *Determine readiness for next course at completion of each term*
  - Internship begins first semester of year three
    - Two courses for internship, yearlong, part time
      - *Assess progress mid-term and end of term*
      - *Determine readiness for second course at completion of each term*

Assessment data should be collected by all relevant stakeholders. This includes faculty teaching content courses, the site supervisor, university supervisor, and intern. Therefore, each party needs to be oriented with the assessment tool(s) being used, expectations for completing them, and responsibilities for providing feedback.

Utilizing Online Platforms for Record Keeping

Long gone are the days when documents and records can only be kept in paper file folders, locked in cabinets. While that is certainly still an option, digital platforms have transformed record keeping, documentation storage, hours tracking, and assessment tasks for coordinators, supervisors, and students. Videoconferencing and secure cloud-based systems enable supervisors and interns to connect across geographic distances, facilitating timely feedback and ongoing support (McCarthy, 2020). This section will not specifically espouse one platform to use but rather highlight the growing trend in using online platforms, which documents can be tracked, and considerations for choosing online platforms.

Records that coordinators disseminate and keep track of include, but may not be limited to:

- Supervision agreements
- Handbook signatures
- Liability insurance
- Site agreements
- Hour logs
- Clinical assessments and evaluations
- KPI, SLO, PLO assessments
- Accreditation assessment documents
- Verification of training
- Assignments (as relevant)

Prior to online platforms, coordinators and supervisors collected paper copies, accumulating a significant number of materials that consumed ample storage space. Additionally, coordinators and supervisors were tasked with creating templates for each of these items. Also, when collaborating with stakeholders, disseminating and collecting documents could be nuanced and fraught with issues. Electronic platforms have streamlined record-keeping and administrative tasks, reducing paperwork and improving organization (Watson & Hill, 2023).

While efficiency is advantageous, challenges can arise from securing funds to purchase the platform and in transitioning from paper to digital formats. Additionally, as with any technology mechanism, there will be issues that arise either sporadically or continuously with accessing all features of the platform, training individuals on how to use it, and a variety of other technology, internet, and access issues.

Selecting a digital platform for record keeping involves evaluating your organization's needs, workflows, and regulatory requirements. Essential features to look for include customizable templates, secure storage, efficient dissemination and collection tools, and robust security measures such as encryption and role-based access. The platform should support integration with existing systems and provide user-friendly interfaces to ensure that coordinators, supervisors, and stakeholders can easily transition from paper to digital processes.

Potential challenges include technology access issues, confidentiality concerns, and the need for robust training on platform use (Bain & Jones, 2021). Usability and quality training resources are vital, as is the platform's ability to scale and adapt over time. Effective supervision via digital platforms depends on secure, user-friendly interfaces and clear protocols for handling sensitive information. Additionally, fostering strong supervisory relationships may require intentional efforts to maintain engagement and rapport in virtual environments (Lenz & Smith, 2022).

Financial considerations, including both initial and ongoing costs, are crucial, especially as funding constraints can hinder adoption. It's also important to anticipate challenges in migrating records, training users, and troubleshooting technology issues. Engaging stakeholders in the selection process, piloting platforms before full implementation, and prioritizing features that directly address your most frequent administrative tasks will help ensure a smooth and effective transition to a digital record-keeping system.

Ongoing Review of Fieldwork

Evaluating the efficacy of the fieldwork program is a critical, ongoing process that ensures students are gaining the practical experience, skills, and professional competencies required by both regulatory standards and the demands of their future professions. A robust evaluation plan should integrate both quantitative and qualitative data sources, drawing from hour logs, clinical assessments, KPI/SLO/PLO assessments, supervisor feedback, and student reflections.

To systematically assess program outcomes, a structured schedule should be established. At the start of each academic year, baseline data from prior cohorts can be reviewed to set benchmarks for success. Mid-term assessments—conducted at the semester's halfway point—allow coordinators and supervisors to identify emerging trends or concerns, enabling timely interventions. Comprehensive end-of-term evaluations should aggregate data from all fieldwork sites, capturing insights about placement quality, student skill development, and areas for program growth.

Beyond these routine cycles, annual reviews of fieldwork outcomes against accreditation standards and program goals help ensure alignment and continuous improvement. Incorporating periodic stakeholder feedback—through surveys and focus groups—fosters a culture of responsiveness, allowing adjustments to be made in response to changing student needs, site requirements, or broader shifts in the field. By adhering to a defined evaluation schedule and emphasizing transparency and adaptability, programs can continuously refine the quality and impact of their fieldwork experiences, ultimately supporting both student success and institutional excellence.

Site Placements

While CACREP (2024) standards require programs to provide students with guidance on securing placements, they don't require coordinators or university supervisors to complete the placements for students. Either opportunity provides benefits and considerations for all parties involved.

Coordinators Securing Placements

Coordinators work in advance from either a determined list or growing list of potential sites to place students at the required number or types of sites to complete the required experiences as listed in both professional practice and specific professional identity standards. This may include setting up interviews with site supervisors and interns in systematic group formats or individually. This gives coordinators a degree of control to "match make" students with supervisors and sites that will be mutually beneficial and provide optimal learning and growth opportunities. This also allows coordinators to foster strong collaborative relationships with sites and supervisors ongoingly.

If a site placement falls through due to supervisors leaving their place of employment, no longer being able to take interns, or other circumstances, coordinators work immediately in response to find a new placement. This approach is advantageous in that it gives the coordinator advanced control over ensuring fieldwork sites are legitimate for the required experiences, supervisors have necessary and ongoing training, and developed relationships that will support the program and students comprehensively.

A primary consideration is the time involved in placements. For example, different professional identities require different fieldwork experiences. A mental health counseling intern may only need one site, and the placement work is not extensive. When placing 12–24, or so, students, the work may be moderate. For school counseling students, who need experience at all levels K-12, interns may need three sites. Placing 12–24 students at two to three sites individually is an extensive amount of work. Additionally, when placements fall through shortly before a term begins or mid-term, the coordinator acts in almost a crisis response manner to place interns as quickly as possible. Lastly, for fully online programs, coordinators will have less capacity for coordinating placements long-distance and there can be difficulties that arise from not being familiar with the community or systems in which the intern lives in.

Students Securing Placements

Students work in advance, within a specific timeline and predetermined deadlines, to secure the number of placements at the required locations, to complete fieldwork requirements. The coordinators degree of involvement can vary from providing pre-approved lists, to working alongside during the placement seeking process, to being less involved until the placement is secure. This approach provides students with the opportunity to network within their communities and practice professional skills to secure their placement. Coordinators will ensure sites can provide students with required learning and experiences, supervisors are eligible to supervise and receive orientation about the fieldwork experience and counseling program.

This work can be less intensive than placing each student. Students who are lacking in self-efficacy and professionalism skills may struggle to complete this task on their own, may fail at meeting deadlines, and the coordinator may need to intervene late in the process to ensure students secure a placement. Additionally, when new sites routinely are added as students find their own placements, the coordinator will be responsible for ensuring the onboarding and orientation processes are complete before fieldwork begins. Whereas with operating from a pre-approved list and/or placing students, with orientation and vetting work already completed, a coordinator will be engaging in several tangential tasks in a potentially short time frame for a site to be ready for a student to begin fieldwork. The work may be less than securing placements but still intricate and time sensitive.

Coordinators will consider what is best practice based on the geographical, community, cultural, program, professional identity, and developmental needs of students to decide if the degree of involvement for placement. In either approach, coordinators are responsible for nurturing relationships with sites and supervisors which is essential for the counseling programs and students.

Fundamental Features of Coordination

Coordinators and university supervisors are faced with a myriad of ongoing tasks and responsibilities. Below we detail many of those tasks.

Training Site Supervisors

Site supervisors are to receive ongoing opportunities for training. Topics are endless related to clinical practice, supervision practice, technology use, and relevant professional topics. Coordinators will benefit from surveying their site supervisors to identify emerging needs. Opportunities can include direct training from the coordinator or other faculty, links to online or in-person training, and disseminating resources. Additionally, site supervisors need to be oriented on the program's expectations, requirements, and evaluation processes per accreditation standards. Coordinators can consider developing materials that can be used continuously, in digital formats, for efficient procedures in orientation training. We encourage coordinators to think in advance for a systematic approach, with both prescribed and responsive training topics, to engage supervisors in continuing education and training efforts.

Site Visits

Site visits are not required by accreditation but are still a common practice for counseling programs. If the coordinator is not teaching the fieldwork course, it is not recommended they conduct the site visit due to disconnects with the intern and site supervisor. The university supervisor, who has been involved with the interns, should be the one to complete the visit. The coordinator can determine the process for the visit: when it occurs, if it is virtual or in-person, if live supervision of practice will happen, evaluation efforts during the visit, and system for meeting with intern and supervisor.

Communication with Site Supervisors

The 2024 CACREP standards specify in Section 4, standard J

During entry-level professional practice experiences, the counselor education program engages in consultation with the fieldwork site supervisor to monitor student learning and performance in accordance with the supervision agreement.

In previous standard cycles, the requirement was for bi-weekly communication with site supervisors during the practicum phase. With this change, there is an open framework for coordinators to determine the process for communication with site supervisors. Both the coordinator and university supervisor can communicate via email or phone calls. The communication can include updates about what is being discussed in university supervision, what site supervisors can be focusing on for the stage of development interns are in, upcoming considerations, supervision tips and tools, and an array of other relevant items. The communication can be prescriptive or in response to emerging themes in supervision or feedback from needs assessments given to site supervisors. We encourage deliberate, routine, and efficient methods for communication and consultation.

Supporting University Supervisors

Whether coordinating in small or large programs, coordinators consider their process for working with university supervisors, who may be faculty, adjuncts, or doctoral students. The needs of each party may vary greatly or be similar to one another. Consultation, supervision of supervision, and collaboration are paramount to effective fieldwork programs. We encourage coordinators to determine a routine approach for working with university supervisors individually and as a group (as needed).

Considerations within Professional Identities

Coordinators benefit from awareness of specific facets within different professional identities. Coordinators and university supervisors may be working with students from the same professional identity, and it is always possible to be working with students from a different professional identity. Supervision groups may be a cohort of the same professional identity or a mix of identities. Doctoral students who supervise may have zero experience with the professional identity of the interns. Therefore, we will provide some beginning insights into the different complexities.

School Counseling

School counselors work collaboratively with administrators, teachers, school staff, students, and families. School counselors are considered leaders in their school system. Their primary population is minors, which requires attention to legal and ethical codes for this age group. Emphasis is placed on working in systems both in the school and within the community the school resides in, school climate, and the interconnection between academic, career, and social-emotional. Interns will be working with federal and state regulations and laws regarding education practices and rights. To obtain experience at all levels, interns will likely be at two to three sites during traditional working hours. Site supervisors will be licensed but are not required by state to have supervisor training for their school counseling role. Relevant organizations for further resources include The American School Counselor Association and Association for Child and Adolescent Counseling.

Mental Health and Addictions Counseling

Mental health counselors work in a variety of settings ranging from out-patient, intensive outpatient, to in-patient environments. In addition to clinical skills, knowledge, and behaviors listed in the accreditation standards, students are learning the interplay between insurance companies and mental health parity. They will be learning the state codes for their scope of practice and other systemic influences on their clinical work. Addictions professionals are also learning the laws and state codes that impact scope of services, health insurance coverage for inpatient and out-patient services, and other community systems that impact rehabilitation (law enforcement, medical services, psychiatric care). There is a strong emphasis on community partnerships, collaboration with health care professionals, and advocacy for parity of services. Site supervisors will have a license and may or may not have supervisor training depending on state and organization requirements for their role. Relevant organizations for further resources include the American Counseling Association, the American Mental Health Counselors Association, the National Association for Addiction Professionals, and the International Association of Addictions and Offender Counselors.

College and Student Affairs and Career Counseling

College and student affairs and career counseling professionals work in community, organizational and higher education environments in a variety of settings from academic success, career centers, cultural and diversity offices, first-generation and non-traditional student centers, Greek life, residence halls, and student services departments. Interns will be learning about federal, state, and campus laws, policies, and codes that affect students' rights and access to education. They are learning about administration systems and how campus departments work with campus-wide leaders and state governing boards. Additionally, there is strong emphasis on the community, campus climate, and systems involved in an individual's life. As well, they consider the roles that advocacy and social justice have in equitable access to education and career services. Licensure is not required in many student affairs and career services roles, nor is supervisor training. Coordinators will need to verify relevant active certifications and supervisor training needs. Obtaining direct hours may not be as inherently available given the varied nature of direct services across the different higher education systems, and interning at multiple sites is an important consideration. Relevant organizations for further resources include the American College Personnel Association, American College Counseling Association, National Employment Counseling Association, and National Career Development Association.

Clinical Rehabilitation and Rehabilitation Counseling

Professionals in rehabilitation counseling work to support individuals with varying levels of disabilities. Emphasis is on supporting clients' vocationally with housing services, career services, supporting basic living needs, and navigating community systems to understand barriers that may exist for clients with disabilities that impede one's ability to thrive. Sites may include federal or state government organizations. With licensure and education needs for these roles varying, coordinators will need to check with state requirements for licensure and certification when determining if a site supervisor is qualified. Relevant organizations for further resources include the American Rehabilitation Counseling Association and the National Rehabilitation Counseling Association.

Marriage, Couple, and Family Counseling

In addition to similar considerations for state codes and laws, health care access and mental health parity from the other mental health counseling identities, professionals in this field are working with the complexity and impact of relevant community systems that impact each individual in a couple and family unit. Working with families may mean internship sites that are open after traditional 9-5 settings to accommodate for work and school schedules. Sites may include non-traditional settings such as shelters and rehabilitation centers. Site supervisors will have a license in this field and may or may not have had supervisor training. Relevant organizations for further resources include the International Association of Marriage and Family Counselors and the American Association for Marriage and Family Therapy.

Counselor Education and Supervision

Doctoral interns are preparing for future roles in advanced clinical work, higher education, and supervisory roles. Fieldwork sites should be specific to future work and can include assistant teaching with faculty, supervising master's level interns, specialized clinical and counseling settings, and research assistantships. Some universities provide on-site clinics for master's students to complete practicum and internship hours. Those programs, with doctoral programs, can utilize doctoral students in clinical supervisor roles. We address this option further in the chapter on legal and ethical considerations. These interns will need ample orientation and training for their supervision work. Supervision of their supervision work is a critical fieldwork element. Doctoral interns may be collecting hours toward a clinical license during their internship work, as well. Coordinators will critically examine the licenses and credentials of the site supervisor to determine if they are qualified not only by CACREP standards, but also per state licensing board standards. Relevant organizations for further resources include the Association for Counselor Education and Supervision and the Association of Counselors, Counselor Educators, Supervisors, and Students.

Fieldwork Coordinator's Checklist

Essential Tasks for Effective Oversight

This checklist was developed by the author with considerations for accreditation standards.

General Coordination

- Develop a manual/handbook compliant with accreditation standards that is routinely reviewed and updated
- Determine a schedule for a comprehensive program evaluation of the fieldwork program.
- Confirm fieldwork sites align with students' counseling specialization (e.g., mental health, college and student affairs, clinical rehabilitation, marriage and family, counselor education).
- Ensure site supervisors hold relevant licenses and certifications as required by state, federal, and accreditation standards.
- Verify site supervisors' training in supervision, if applicable for the setting and role.
- Confirm that internship sites comply with all relevant state, federal, campus, and organizational codes, laws, and policies.
- Review internship site operation hours to accommodate students' and clients' needs (e.g., non-traditional hours for marriage and family counseling).
- Assess the availability of direct service hours and consider multiple-site placements if necessary.
- Determine the frequency for collecting hour logs and verifying students are on track to complete all required hours and types of experiences

Student Preparation and Support

- Ensure students have a clear understanding of their scope of practice, state codes, and systemic influences on clinical work.
- Provide orientation on insurance companies, mental health parity, and coverage for different counseling services.

- Educate students about administrative and campus systems, advocacy, and social justice issues relevant to their specialty.
- Guide students in navigating community systems (law enforcement, medical services, housing, etc.) where applicable.
- Support students' engagement with professional organizations for ongoing resources and development.

Site Supervisor Assessment

- Verify licensure and credentials of site supervisors and ensure compliance with both CACREP and state board standards.
- Confirm supervisor training requirements based on state and organizational policies.
- Check for active certifications or credentials.

Fieldwork Structure and Oversight

- Design intentional fieldwork sequences and experiences that meet accreditation standards and address legal/ethical codes.
- Facilitate collaboration between students, supervisors, and community/healthcare professionals.
- Leverage technology for organization, tracking, and support throughout fieldwork.
- Provide ample orientation and ongoing training for doctoral interns in supervision roles.
- Ensure supervision of supervision work for doctoral interns and support hour accrual toward licensure where applicable.

Professional Engagement and Resources

- Connect students and supervisors with relevant professional organizations (e.g., American Counseling Association, National Career Development Association, American Rehabilitation Counseling Association, etc.).
- Encourage student's and site supervisor's participation in professional development activities and resource utilization.

Conclusion

Coordinating fieldwork programs require intentionality, organization, and an adherence to accreditation standards and relevant legal and ethical codes. By thoughtfully designing experiences, supporting both students and site supervisors, and leveraging technology, fieldwork coordinators can ensure that emerging professionals are well-prepared to meet the evolving needs of the field. The fieldwork coordinator plays a crucial role in ensuring that interns are placed in appropriate settings that align with their area of counseling specialization. They are responsible for verifying that site supervisors and internship sites meet all relevant state, federal, and certification requirements, as well as ensuring that students gain exposure to the necessary laws, policies, and codes that govern professional practice. Lastly, they also foster connections with professional organizations for further resources and professional development.

References

Bain, K., & Jones, D. (2021). Digital platforms in clinical record keeping: Challenges and considerations. *Journal of Counseling Administration, 34*(2), 112–128.

Council for Accreditation of Counseling and Related Educational Programs (CACREP). (2024). *2024 Standards*. Retrieved from https://www.cacrep.org/for-programs/2024-cacrep-standards/

Lenz, A. S., & Smith, T. B. (2022). Supervision in digital environments: Fostering engagement and safeguarding confidentiality. *Journal of Counseling Administration, 35*(3), 201–219.

McCarthy, J. (2020). The role of technology in remote supervision: Videoconferencing and cloud-based systems. *Journal of Educational Technology, 36*(2), 123–135.

Watson, J. C., & Hill, N. R. (2023). The impact of electronic platforms on administrative efficiency in clinical education. *Journal of Clinical Administration, 37*(1), 45–59.

CHAPTER 6
SUPERVISION THEORIES AND GROUP SUPERVISION MODELS

Abstract

In this chapter, we overview commonly used supervision theories and available group supervision models. While this is not the expansive list of theories, the ones discussed are commonly discussed in scholarly work and/or used in practice. There is a smaller body of scholarly work on group supervision models, and we reference several in this chapter. The focus of this chapter is not to convince the reader that theories are based on evidence or have efficacy. Rather, the focus is on encouraging the reader (anticipated faculty supervisor) to be deliberate in choosing a theoretical lens and guiding model to be effective in their work. After discussing theories and models, we provide a decision-making model for the reader to use to understand the process of infusing theory with models, into practice.

Counseling Supervision

Bernard and Goodyear (2019) define supervision as, "an intervention provided by a more senior member of a profession to a more junior member or members of that same profession" (pg. 9). That intervention is evaluative, long-term, and has different purposes related to ensuring that the supervisee is developing and performing adequately enough so that future clients will benefit from their counseling work. Within an academic framework, as guided by accreditation standards, supervisees receive at least two types of this intervention: in the classroom and on site with their field placement site supervisor. It is essential to recognize that this gatekeeping process and corresponding intervention are inherently integrated with pre-service education and training.

DOI: 10.4324/9781003356776-7

In counseling interventions, procedures are not conducted at random. Counselors use evidence-based practices informed by counseling or psychotherapy theories, which may follow a treatment plan or model. Similarly, supervision involves intervention work that is guided by theory, evidence, and structured frameworks or plans. Since supervision is considered an intervention, unsystematic supervision does not occur in this context. Supervision theories and models provide structure and support for the responsibilities handled by supervisors. Developing skills for effective integration of theory and framework in counseling takes time. As such, supervision is generally provided by more experienced professionals who assist less experienced members in building their professional identity, enhancing skills, and combining personal and professional aspects as counselors. With that acknowledgment, we know that university supervisors may be at varying points in their professional experiences.

Group supervision in academic settings can be challenging or rewarding, depending on perspective. This text examines group supervision models and offers a brief overview of relevant theories for supervisors and supervisees. The complexity arises from integrating group supervision models with supervision theory, all within an academic environment and alongside group dynamics (covered in the next chapter). There is limited scholarly guidance on combining these components. Rather than seeking perfection, the goal is to understand the key elements and maintain fidelity in supervision interventions. The chapter will further clarify these elements.

Overview of Supervision Theories

Bernard and Goodyear (2019) discuss supervision models in their widely recognized work, which is accepted by certain supervisory credentialing organizations as a key resource for fulfilling educational requirements. They classify these supervision models into three main categories: Models grounded in psychotherapy theory, developmental approaches, and social role models. That list is, however, not exhaustive, and further researching and investigating will yield more models not discussed in the textbook. For the sake of continuity with the espoused text on the topic, we will overview these categories in this chapter. Lastly, as Bernard and Goodyear (2019) also point out in their text, there are entire books dedicated to just one supervision theory addressed. Regarding fidelity in implementing a theory or model, readers will need to consider additional training in any theory they wish to use. The focus of this chapter is to increase awareness for the imperative of using theory to avoid faculty supervisors intervening in happenstance, haphazard manners.

Psychotherapy Theory

Scholars recognize that supervision could be dated as far back as 1902 when novice doctors sought to learn psychoanalysis from Sigmund Freud, with the credit given to Freud being the first supervisor (Harkness & Poertner, 1989; Freud, 1986; Jacobs et al., 1995). Psychodynamic supervision embodies concepts of the working alliance and parallel process, both of which are also foundational to psychodynamic counseling work. Psychotherapeutic approaches are a combination of teaching and learning that focus intently on the relationships between the client, counselor (intern), supervisor (faculty) and their interconnectedness (Ekstein & Wallerstein, 1972). The teaching focuses on working closely with the counselor in training to aid them in understanding the mechanics of working through relational conflicts between the supervisor and counselor in training (Bernard & Goodyear, 2019).

Like psychotherapy, the supervisor takes on a role that is not focused on being an expert in theory and technique, but rather on being a participant in the supervisory process, using relational aspects to influence the process. There are several approaches within psychotherapy-based supervision. These approaches will strongly consider the relationship between the supervisor and counselor in training (CIT), and how that relationship influences the developmental work of supervision. The work can focus on the client, the CIT, or the relationship between the supervisor and CIT. The supervisor is to be mindful of their stance, position of power and how it is used, and how they cultivate a relationship with their CIT to create supportive dynamics that will lead toward growth experiences for the CIT.

Below are theoretical approaches within psychotherapeutic housing, with brief descriptions. Again, this is not an exhaustive list but one to highlight common approaches and the different conceptualization that the theories have.

Person Centered *(Hackney & Goodyear, 1984)*

Places strong emphasis on helping the supervisee grow in their confidence, increase self-awareness, and conceptualization of the therapeutic process. The Supervisor incorporates elements of teaching and therapy to guide the supervisee toward self-actualization.

Cognitive Behavioral *(Boyd, 1978; Bradley & Olson, 1980; Milne & James, 2000)*

Provides a structured framework for supervisors to utilize that focuses on the supervisee's progress specifically about appropriate therapist behaviors and skills. The goal is to eliminate inappropriate behaviors and increase appropriate ones. The supervisor utilizes teaching and training to assist in the acquisition of identified skills and their subsequent applications.

Constructivist *(Bernard & Goodyear, 2019)*

Recognizes that truth and reality are constructed within each individual based on their social interactions. Emphasis is placed on the individual's subjective experience. Language is focused on for its use in constructing subjective reality. A supervisor strives for equality with the supervisee and focuses on supervisee strengths.

Narrative *(Clifton et al., 1990)*

This approach also recognizes relativism and truth. Emphasis is on story telling with the supervisor aiding the supervisee in analyzing the client's life story while also helping the supervisee develop their own professional story. The editorial work that the supervisor conducts focuses on the stories that supervisees tell of themselves, their clients, and of other clinicians. Supervisors take a stance of curiosity and utilize basic skills of open-ended questions and reflections as they process the stories.

Solution Focused *(Juhnke, 1996)*

This approach does not focus on processing or analyzing in traditional psychoanalytical ways but is instead focused on problem resolution and goal attainment. The supervisor helps the supervisee identify and lean into their own strengths and resources to make changes with autonomy. The supervisor focuses on building a supportive relationship to avoid or work around resistance from the supervisee. In skill building and competency development, supervisors will have supervisee focus on strengths and success-as opposed to faults, whilst working toward small and obtainable goals.

Developmental Approaches

Developmental models of supervision focus on growth and change in a supervisee's capacity over time as they train and receive supervision. These methods acknowledge comprehensive elements that can be addressed by supervisors and supervisees. Developmental approaches commonly used are the Integrated Developmental Model, The Rønnestad and Skovholt Model, and the Loganbill, Hardy, and Delworth Model. Supervisors take on different roles in their supervisory work to be responsive and supportive as they nurture their supervisees through their stages of development. Supervisors maintain a goal to shape their supervision to meet the unique needs of supervisees at any given stage. Developmental approaches consider stages of capacity and competency. These stages are directional, sequential and conceptualize that overtime supervisees will evolve as they pass through the stages with increased capability and competency in their clinical work, professionalism, and personhood.

Developmental approaches maintain specific guiding assumptions. The first is that supervisees' needs will change as they gain experience and acquire new skills. Because of that assumption, supervisors know they will need to adjust their approaches to be responsive to the changing developmental needs of their supervisees. Supervision work considers the holistic factors (emotional, cognitive, and behavioral) as well as the personal and professional growth needs of supervisees. The supervisor takes on different roles to meet the needs by being flexible and supportive. Therefore, feedback, teaching, and mentoring are not prescriptive but rather responsive. These models may have the most potential in academic settings due to their focus on sequencing and emphasis on teaching and learning. However, as supervisors have learned in their introductory counseling classes, all theories can work to the extent that they can work and therefore any approach has promise when utilized intentionally.

Integrated Developmental Model *(Stoltenberg & Delworth, 1987)*

This model describes development through three levels with three over-arching constructs that are used in assessing professional growth. Those constructs are self-other awareness, motivation, and autonomy. There are eight domains for professional development: intervention skills competence, assessment techniques, interpersonal assessment, client conceptualization, individual differences, theoretical orientation, treatment plans and goals, and professional ethics. Level one is the beginner stage in which supervisees are more reliant on direct guidance, supportive feedback, and exhibit the most anxiety. Level two supervisees show more confidence and independence, employing more autonomy but still need intentional guidance in refining their skills and comprehensive counseling work. Level three is defined as advanced in which supervisees are actualizing with the three constructs and supervision is more collective and collaborative.

Rønnestad and Skovholt *(Rønnestad & Skovholt, 1993; 2003)*

This approach was developed and vetted with graduate level internship students and is a life-span developmental model that has six phases that supervisees pass through. Some of the stages are post-graduation with the auspice that supervision is encouraged to be life-long.

- Phase 1: Lay Helper: Interns display basic and underdeveloped skills. They are more prone to boundary issues and inappropriate affect in their helping work.
- Phase 2: Beginning Student: Interns are eager to "get it right" and very sensitive toward critical feedback. An impressionable time for learning all the facets related to the counseling work they are doing.
- Phase 3: The Advanced Student: Interns are performing at higher adequate levels and acquiring more skills, developing a stronger professional identity, and potentially taking on more leadership in supervision with their peers. Interns are still self-conscious about performing correctly but may have more confidence and comfort.
- Phase 4: The Novice Professional: Post-graduation counseling work in which the intern, now a professional counselor, continues to solidify their counseling identity, grow in their capacities, and seeks a position congruent with their identity.

- Phase 5: The Experienced Professional: Counselors are skilled, experienced, and focus more intentionally on the therapeutic alliance and its leverage for the counseling process.
- Phase 6: The Senior Professional: Identified as having at least 20 years of experience. Counselors are judicious about changing their approaches and show more humility in their work. Counselors may find themselves contributing to the field's growth and development.

Loganbill, Hardy, and Delworth (1982)

One of the first comprehensive developmental models that contains three stages, eight supervisory issues, and supervisor interventions to help supervisees move through the stages.

Stage one is stagnation in which the supervisee is not progressing on their own and requires more help from the supervisor. They need help building their self-efficacy.

Stage two is confusion and characterized as an awkward growth time in which supervisees are freeing themselves from rigid constraints but are overwhelmed with all the forces, learning, and content they are engaging with. They are moving toward independence and their recognition that the supervisor will be less involved can cause negative emotions and behaviors.

Stage three is integration and reflective of supervisees working through their growing pains. They are advancing in their skills, taking responsibility and initiative, and growing in self-efficacy. The relationship with the supervisor is more balanced and supervisees are realistic about what to expect from their supervisors.

The eight issues include supervisory relationship, competence, emotional awareness, purpose and direction, autonomy, personal, respect for individual differences, professional ethics, motivation, and identity.

Discrimination Model (Bernard, 1997)

Widely used in counseling supervision, this model provides a structured framework to guide supervisors in responding to the changing needs of their supervisees. The term discriminate refers to a supervisor's ability to identify the skills and tasks required by the supervisee at any given time during supervision. The supervisor embodies three roles: teacher, counselor, and consultant. They focus on three specific skill areas: intervention, conceptualization, and personalization. Like other developmental models, the supervisor is encouraged to be flexible and mold their work based on the supervisee's levels of capacity and competence. Supervision is tailored, responsive, and deliberate. Unlike developmental models, there are no identified stages or phases in which supervisees are expected to pass through. Rather, supervisors will focus on assessing strengths and needs, provide targeted interventions to address needs or deficiencies, and create a supportive environment that can foster holistic growth for supervisees.

Moving Ahead

These models discussed, aside from the Rønnestad and Skovholt (2003) model, are not specifically focused on group supervision nor supervision in an academic setting. These models have highlighted the personal characteristics in supervisees that impact the relationship, work, and needs in supervision. Consider a group of 12 students, which is the CACREP maximum ratio of students to faculty in a supervision course, and all the complexities happening within the individuals and group. Additionally, consider the intensity of the work espoused in these models toward not just one individual but toward 12 individuals. That is quite a lot of work to take on. The engineering work of infusing a supervision theory with a group supervision model is a tricky task but a guiding model is provided at the end of this chapter.

Group Supervision Models

Group supervision is widely practiced across various fields beyond academia. As noted previously, opportunities for training in group supervision remain limited or are frequently unavailable. The most recent edition of Bernard and Goodyear (2019) incorporates group supervision models that were not included in earlier editions. This chapter will review those models discussed in the text, along with an additional model drawn from recent scholarly literature. It should be noted that the applications of these models within academic contexts are not explicitly outlined in the original sources. Accordingly, this chapter provides examples of how group supervision models can be contextualized with supervision theory in academic settings.

Linton (2005) and Bernard and Goodyear (2019) offer overviews of both the Systemic Peer Group Supervision model (Borders, 1991) and the Structured Group Supervision model (Wilbur et al., 1991). Additionally, the Grounded Theory Model (Fleming et al., 2010) will be examined. Linton (2005) also introduces further models relevant to group supervision, which share foundational frameworks with those discussed here and emphasize case conceptualization as a central process.

Systemic Peer Group Supervision: Structured Group Supervision (Borders, 1991)

This model is known by two different names, as noted in the title above. Its goal is to address unhelpful elements of peer group supervision. This model has specific tasks for the leader and members to follow. Case examples, preferably live examples, are used to guide the group supervision process. The supervisor is the moderator to keep the group focused and on tasks. They also provide feedback about the group dynamics. The supervisor is to be mindful of where the supervisees are at developmentally as they give process feedback and summarize the group feedback session.

Peers are given or can choose a task to take on as they observe or engage with the case study, such as attending to non-verbal behaviors, the use of confrontation, or the use of skills. The second task is to take on a role which can be an observer, the client, the counselor, or someone related to the client. The supervisee will give feedback based on the role they took on. A third task is to observe from a theoretical orientation, which can be one or several individuals, and to assess the session from different theoretical perspectives. The fourth task is for an observer to create a descriptive metaphor after watching the session. This allows for a creative layer to dynamically process what is happening in the session. This model is cognizant of group dynamics, but the supervisor will still need to be trained or educated on group theory and group dynamics.

Structured Group Supervision (Wilbur et al., 1991)

This approach has been considered for use in counselor training programs. This model also provides a format for use case conceptualization and direction for supervisors and supervisees on how to interact. There are five phases in the supervision process. The group meetings are intended to be about one hour, which is less than the CACREP requirement of a minimum of 1.5 hours weekly for group supervision.

In the first phase a group member presents a case to the group they need help with. In phase two, the members clarify the needs and obtain more information about the case. Phase three is when members provide relevant feedback and guidance. In phase four, the supervisee determines if the feedback was responsive and helpful. The fifth phase is optional and is when the four phases are processed. The supervisor is flexible in how they process the feedback, frame the presenting issue, and validate the feedback. They are also encouraged to note the group dynamics that are occurring.

Grounded Theory Model (Fleming et al., 2010)

This model emerged from a grounded theory, consensual qualitative research study conducted with counseling psychology doctoral students and supervisors. This model conceptualizes group dynamics, interpersonal and intrapersonal factors occurring in the group supervision space, with the central tendency of *safety* being the most critical element. The conceptualization identifies factors that threaten safety (group conflict, anxiety, defensiveness) and factors that promote safety (cohesion, discussion of group process, fluid leadership, openness, and vulnerability). When a supervisee is feeling threatened, they are more likely to maintain a focus on skills and techniques, with compromised learning. Whereas if a supervisee feels safe, they engage in a more broad-based learning about therapy with a positive impact on their self-awareness and awareness of others that promotes positive vicarious learning.

The more unsafe a supervisee feels, the more disengaged they become, and learning is perceived to be minimal. Group activities, such as case presentation, session review, and didactic learning are encouraged as supervisors consider hinderances to the group process (absenteeism, distractions, time issues, etc.). This model is perceived to have the most promise for an academic setting and is inclusive of the group dynamics we address in the following chapter. Additionally, it is reflective of previously discussed supervision theories such as psychotherapeutic, person-centered, and developmental models.

Infusing Supervision Theory in Group Models

When theory and technique join forces, it can be said that the best practices will emerge. Random supervision happens when supervisors rely on faulty methods such as role modeling because of their perceived expertise, ineffective storytelling, and non-deliberate and ungrounded approaches in their supervision work. The construction work of infusing a theory into a model can be trickier than anticipated. The constraints of the time certain academic terms can make the tricky task even more complicated. Therefore, we will provide a crosswalk example for infusing a theory into a model so that the reader can gain a sense of how to do that on their own.

Application of Supervision Models and Supervision Theory in Classroom Settings

There is not one perfect formula of a theory into a model. The matrix of possibilities can be endless. Rather, the reader will benefit from understanding the process of how to infuse whichever model or theory they choose. Below we provide a step-by-step framework for university supervisors to utilize as they conceptualize the fieldwork course they will teach. The best practice would be to do the design work before the term in which the course is being taught begins.

Step 1: Determine the supervisory goals. Will you focus more intently on:

- Skill development
- Personal insight and growth
- The supervisory relationship
- Multiple aspects of supervision

Step 2: Identify the supervision theory that most closely aligns with the supervisory goal

- Skills development: Cognitive behavioral, Solution-Focused
- Personal insight and growth: Psychodynamic, Narrative, Constructivist
- The supervisory relationship: Person-centered
- Multiple aspects of supervision: Developmental models, Discrimination model

Step 3: Consider a group supervision model that is congruent with the academic environment and coursework needs.

Additionally, supervisors need to think critically about how the supervisory goals and supervision theory will align with the academic needs and group supervision model. Supervision theory concerns itself with how the supervisor engages with the individual they are supervising. Group models concern themselves with the functioning of the group, less about the theory behind why supervisors behave the way they do. Some models may not lend themselves to specific theories as well as others might.

Systemic Peer Group Supervision

The Systemic Peer Group Supervision's model relies primarily on peer-to-peer interactions due to its emphasis on using peers in structured roles to give critical feedback on case studies. This approach requires the supervisor to attend to group dynamics in a mindful manner, paying attention to the elements that interfere with group cohesion building. While the supervisor certainly considers their relationship with the group, the focus is more-so on the group's relationship with one another. Person-centered theory may work with this model, but the supervisor needs to consider the relationships from multiple viewpoints: supervisor to supervisee, supervisor to the group, supervisee to supervisee. Solution-focused, cognitive behavioral, and skill focused theoretical approaches may also work well with this model, but the supervisor must also pay attention to group dynamics as they focus on utilizing peers for skill development.

Structured Group Supervision

Structured group supervision also utilizes a case study approach for conceptualizing the group supervision time. The five phases give explicit direction for how to utilize the time allotted for the case processing. While the model dictates what members of the group are doing, it leaves some room for the supervisor to consider how members give feedback or what the feedback can focus on. As the presenting member clarifies their needs, the supervisor can essentially utilize any theory when they engage with the supervisee. They can specifically address what the supervisee wants to focus on. Or, if they are sensing something else is happening or needs focus, they can shift the direction of the feedback. This allows for focus on skills, relationships, self-awareness, or other learning needs. There is a perceived amount of flexibility in what theory a supervisor can utilize in this model ranging from psychoanalytical to developmental models. At the same time, supervisors need to be conscientious of addressing what the supervisee states they need. This requires flexibility of the supervisor to address and meet the needs. Failure to do so can be corrosive to the supervisory relationship with the individual and the group. Members who feel their needs won't be met are susceptible to behaviors that cause the group to become dysfunctional.

Grounded Theory

The Grounded Theory model is quite intricate as it considers personal factors, group dynamics, and academic learning needs. The model focuses inherently on the cognitive factor of safety. The leader has a significant amount of responsibility in promoting dynamics that lead to a member feeling safe. Person-centered approaches would be indivisible in that work of creating an atmosphere for members to reach a point of feeling safe that will foster the desired learning with utilizing case consultation or session reviews. Once the group reaches what is called the "working stage" of the group process, the faculty can find themselves using any of the supervision theories to guide the learning process, with developmental models being very useful (Tuckman & Jensen, 1977). To adequately utilize this model with supportive theoretical approaches, a faculty needs to also be adequately trained in group theory because their group leadership will be the most significant factor in establishing the environment needed within this model. For that reason, the following chapter is focused on group theory in supervision groups.

Step 4: Design the Academic Course and Learning Components

Emphasis on this component is found in Chapter 2

A reasonable goal is to start by simply asking oneself, what kind of supervisor do I want to be? What do I want the group to experience because of me, alongside of me, and with each other? These philosophical questions are a starting point in the process and one ought to remember that it cannot all be changed overnight, it takes time—just as it did with the clinical counseling work. After self-reflecting on these questions and answers, the reader can embark on creating a vision for the fieldwork course with an aim to implement one or two new pieces in their work—whether starting brand new or building upon previous work. A final recommendation is to seek mentoring or supervision for the supervision work that will be done. Supervision of supervision is an invaluable practice to refine the work being done.

Table 6.1 can be used to guide supervisors in selecting an appropriate supervision theory and group supervision model based on the needs of their group, the learning objectives, and the desired group dynamics. Supervisors should reflect on their own philosophy, the needs of their supervisees, and the academic context before making a final decision.

TABLE 6.1	Decision-Making Table for Supervision Theory and Group Supervision Model		
Supervision Model	**Recommended Supervision Theories**	**Key Considerations**	**When to Choose**
Systemic Peer Group Supervision	Person-centered, Solution-focused, Cognitive Behavioral, Skill-focused	Focus on peer-to-peer interaction, group dynamics, and multiple relationship viewpoints	When peer feedback and skill development are priorities, and group cohesion is essential
Structured Group Supervision	Flexible (Psychoanalytical, Developmental, Person-centered, etc.)	Explicit direction, case study approach, flexibility in feedback focus, responsiveness to supervisee needs	When structure is needed, but flexibility in theory application is desired; supporting individual learning needs within a group
Grounded Theory Group Supervision	Person-centered, Developmental, Cognitive Behavioral	Emphasis on psychological safety, group dynamics, and academic learning; requires strong group leadership skills	When fostering a safe group environment and supporting academic growth are critical; leader is trained in group theory

Conclusion

We cover a lot of ground in this chapter, groundwork that is also addressed externally in large volumes of research articles, textbooks, and scholarly work. The emphasis on supplemental training in supervision cannot be lost, as it is also required to some degree by accreditation standards and state licensing boards. Feeling overwhelmed by the weaving work of theories and models is understandable and normal. Just as when we entered the field of counseling and aimed to utilize a theoretical orientation, it can feel challenging and unattainable at times. Therefore, becoming skilled at the weaving work takes time and requires being deliberate. If this is the first time the reader even considered that a theory and group model, in addition to the group theory learning that comes in the next chapter, could (should) be used in their work, then the reader is already one-step ahead in their work.

References

Bernard, J. M. (1997). The discrimination model. In C. E. Watkins (Ed.), *Handbook of psychotherapy supervision* (pp. 310–327). New York, NY: Wiley.

Bernard, J. M., & Goodyear, R. K. (2019). *Fundamentals of clinical supervision* (6th ed.). New York, NY: Pearson.

Borders, L. (1991). A systemic approach to peer group supervision. *Journal of Counseling and Development, 69,* 248–252.

Boyd, J. (1978). *Counselor supervision: Approaches, preparation, practices.* Muncie, IN: Accelerated Development, Inc.

Bradley, J. R., & Olson, J. K. (1980). Training factors influencing felt psycho-therapeutic competence of psychology trainees. *Professional Psychology, 11,* 930–934.

Clifton, D., Doan, R., & Mitchell, D. (1990). The reauthoring of therapist's stories: Taking doses of our own medicine. *Journal of Strategic and Systemic Therapies, 9*(4), 61–66.

Ekstein, R., & Wallerstein, R. S. (1972). *The teaching and learning of psychother-apy* (2nd ed.). New York: International University Press.

Fleming, L. M. et al. (2010). Group process and learning: A grounded theory model of group supervision. *Training and Education in Professional Psy-chology, 4*(3), 194–203.

Freud, S. (1986). On the history of the psychoanalytical movement (first published in 1914). In *Historical and expository works on psychoanalysis.* Harmondsworth: Penguin.

Hackney, H. L., & Goodyear, R. K. (1984). Carl Rogers's client-centered approach to supervision. In R. F. Levant & J. M. Shlien (Eds.). *Client-centered therapy and the person-centered approach: New directions in theory, research, and practice* (pp. 278–296). New York, NY: Praeger.

Harkness, D., & Poertner, A. (1989). Research and social work supervision. *Social Work, 34,* 115–119.

Jacobs, D., David, P., & Meyer, D. J. (1995). *The supervisor encounter: A guide for teachers of psychodynamic psychotherapy and analysis.* New Haven, CT: Yale University Press.

Juhnke, G. A. (1996). Solution-focused supervision: Promoting supervisee skills and confidence through successful solutions. *Counselor Education and Supervision, 36,* 48–57.

Linton, J. M. (2005). Group supervision: A review of practices and models in training. *Dimensions of Counseling, 33*(1), 10–16.

Loganbill, C., Hardy, E., & Delworth, U. (1982). Supervision: A conceptual model. *The Counseling Psychologist, 10,* 3–42.

Milne, D., & James, I. (2000). A systematic review of effective cognitive-behavioral supervision. *British Journal of Clinical Psychology, 41,* 55–72.

Rønnestad, M. H., & Skovholt, T. M. (1993). Supervision of beginning and advanced graduate students of counseling and psychotherapy. *Journal of Counseling & Development, 71,* 396–405.

Rønnestad, M. H., & Skovholt, T. M. (2003). The journey of the counselor and therapist: Research findings and perspectives on professional development. *Journal of Career Development, 30,* 5–44.

Stoltenberg, C., & Delworth, U. (1987). *Supervising counselors and therapists.* San Francisco, CA: Jossey-Bass.

Tuckman, B. W., & Jensen, M. A. C. (1977). Stages of small group development revisited. *Group & Organizational Studies, 2,* 419–427.

Wilbur, M., Roberts-Wilbur, J., Morris, J., Betz, R., & Hart, G. (1991). Structured group supervision: Theory into practice. *Journal for Specialists in Group Work, 16*(2), 91–100.

CHAPTER 7
GROUP THEORY IN GROUP SUPERVISION

Abstract

In this chapter, we reframe how the fieldwork class is viewed. Traditional classroom learning has been didactic and directional, with teacher to student learning. Experiential learning theory and backwards learning design approaches move away from that typical didactic learning to create collective and inclusive learning environments. Those approaches fall into the theories of education and learning. We move in a different direction into group theory to conceptualize the teaching of fieldwork courses. The position is that the supervision group is not a classroom gathering, but rather a group by all standards of the theory. Certainly, inclusive and collaborative methods should be considered within using group theory, but this chapter will focus on what is happening within a supervision group because of the group processes and group procedures. The faculty also considers themselves to be a group leader, interconnected and indivisible from the group process. We discuss the complex dynamics happening simultaneously for the individuals and the group. Additionally, the role of the supervisor group leader is expanded upon.

Conceptualizing the Classroom Group

A class is a group: let this concept permeate. What does that mean for teaching practicum and internship supervision courses? Leaning into group theory and conceptualizing the class as a group transforms nearly everything. There is no longer an individualistic approach in which the faculty solely connects on a 1:1 basis with students. The class becomes a collective approach in which the faculty is working with the students, engaging with the group in different modalities, and acknowledging the microcosmic phenomena of the group that is occurring. When university

DOI: 10.4324/9781003356776-8

supervisors consider group theory, they understand that a group is microcosm of the larger world. Therefore, the work done in the supervision group, as it relates to growth and development, should support an individual's ability to function in the larger group stratosphere of society.

When a fieldwork course faculty adopts a group theory lens, they begin to see beyond the clinical behaviors with clients happening externally. They observe how interns or students interact with peers both individually and in groups, as well as with the faculty supervisor. As many seasoned supervisors know, as the counselor brings "themselves" into the counseling space. Communication, help-seeking, problem solving, dealing with confrontations, and relationship-building skills are demonstrated in these interactions. Nuances or deficiencies in any of the personal areas can impact the counseling efficacy. These interpersonal and intrapersonal skills are quintessential for effective counseling. The question of, "what is the role of the faculty supervisor in addressing group tenants" is quite the large one. This chapter will discuss how to view the supervision group from a group theory lens and group supervision models that can be adopted.

Group Supervision

Group supervision courses are a standard approach in counselor preparation programs. This approach also satisfies the CACREP (2024) requirement for group supervision. Despite it being the standard approach, faculty supervisors will have received little to no training in group supervision methods and practice. Additionally, there is a lack of research on the topics of group theory and group supervision in counseling practicum and internships courses. As Holloway and Johnston have defined, group supervision is a method, "in which supervisors oversee a supervisee's professional development in a group of peers" (1985, pg. 333). Viewing the university course as a group is congruent with the definition. Although group supervision is a topical area covered in the seminal text on supervision by Bernard and Goodyear (2019), the focus is clinical with less emphasis on its application to academic settings. The basis of this chapter is not to espouse the benefits of group supervision, as the Bernard and Goodyear (2019) text discuss. Rather, it is to take a position that as university supervision courses are counted for group supervision, that the faculty teaching the course not only utilize group supervision models but also adopt a group theory lens in their supervision work.

As previously mentioned, accreditation standards specify training areas to be completed, but do not indicate where that training needs to be completed by individuals aspiring to be university-level supervisors. Nor is there a training requirement for group supervision topics. Supervision, however, is a clinical approach and much like with clinical training to become a clinician, the clinical work of supervising benefits from training. Likewise, leading groups and facilitating group counseling requires education and training. With group counseling aspects being a part of accreditation standards at the master's and doctoral level, university supervisors from counseling backgrounds will have a significant amount of knowledge and experience with group theory. Group theory also provides direction for the roles and behaviors of the university supervisor. Therefore, as we adopt a lens comprised of group theory, supervision theory, and group supervision models, there is intricate cross-walking work to be done to provide a faculty supervisor with understanding their role, expectations, and directions to take.

Group Theory

If we start with the end in mind, we ask ourselves, what are students (interns) walking away with because of this group? The emphasis is not on a classroom experience but rather a group experience. The paradox embraced in group counseling is that although there is a prescribed goal (group content), the goal is not actually reaching the goal. While there are many benefits to using groups to support individuals, a larger importance in group approaches is creating a space in which the group is a microcosm of the larger society in which the individuals reside (group process). This microcosm incites individuals to act "as if" they were in the larger society and inspires group process.

Group process is made up of the dynamic forces seen in both larger society and the group microcosm that are outside of the group content. Those forces include emotional regulation, dealing with confrontation, communication skills, relationship building, giving and receiving feedback or critiques, problem resolution, self-efficacy and self-advocacy. This list is not all inclusive but does address many of the forces a group facilitator will encounter with its members. A group facilitator aspires for process to evolve so that they gain a better understanding of the mental and emotional make-up of the participants and thus understand the work that can be done in groups. How does one inspire the process? Content.

Tension exists between the academic requirements of a university supervision course and tenants of group theory. A university supervisor is aware they need to cover the standards that are tied to the course. Interns will be evaluated by those standards in more than one way. Albeit that knowledge, a faculty should think carefully before making the goal achieving the prescribed standards. Why? First, because there is no set requirement for which standards must be addressed in the course. That sets up a subjective and potentially biased approach for determining what students (interns) need to walk away with or be able to do after completing the course. Second, each student is on their own unique developmental journey. Inevitably some of them will be further along in their skills and competencies. To lump them into one trajectory toward the same standard will marginalize the individual, and potentially the group to some extent. While a faculty cannot tailor each element of the content to each individual, they can consider the standards assigned to the course as one target and identify one or more targets for the group to help identify goals. Those additional targets may be designed in the SLOs and KPIs.

Congruent with group theory is to not only identify your goal but to also have the students identify a goal that will drive the content development. Considering that a course needs to be prepared in advance, syllabi need to be finalized, and online course learning modules need to be complete, student driven goals will be a secondary driving force for content. To illustrate the tandem task of creating content before a class begins and concurrently with students, we will utilize the Tuckman and Jensen (1977) group development model, a model that is widely recognized. We will also address group process in conjunction with group content.

Before divulging further, readers must recognize that this chapter is not exhaustive of all that is needed to know about group facilitation and group theory. This chapter will not go significantly deeper into group leadership skills. Readers should spend time becoming more familiar with topics associated with group counseling and group leadership skills by reading texts and materials specifically on those topics. Additionally, as is with group theory, the stages are not always lineal. Only forming and adjourning are promised because each academic term and course has a beginning and ending. We will discuss the group dynamic elements that influence the progression of the stages. Readers, as they become more educated on group counseling and theory will gain deeper introspection into the forces and dynamics that affect moving through stages.

Theoretical Approach to Group Supervision

Pre-Group Planning

Prior to beginning the supervision group, the faculty supervisor engages in pre-group planning work. Other chapters in the book focused on the pre-group elements that faculty and coordinators consider. We will recap some important points from that section. In groups, one can either do pre-screening or intentional selection or have an open format in which members choose their groups. Since we adopt a group theory lens and are cognizant of group dynamics that are affected by relational factors, a coordinator or university faculty will decide if they want to place students intentionally or leave it up to students to pick a faculty or supervision course they want to join.

For programs that have been able to cultivate relationships with students and gain deeper awareness of the holistic personal factors about a student, intentionally placing students into those groups based on their factors can be a beneficial approach. At the same time, bias may interfere with objectively grouping students based on diversity or variety of personal factors. If students self-select there are opportunities for group dynamics that may be either beneficial or challenging. This could look like students who are in cliques or collude with each other, which will lead to potentially problematic moments in group supervision when faculty are providing critical feedback or asking students to engage with each other on deeper levels. Additionally, programs may have someone teaching the course that students have zero experience with and that can cause its own issues with relationship building, trust and rapport, and working cohesively. Either approach will have both positive and negatives. A faculty or a program needs to carefully consider how they form the groups of students.

Less risky areas of the pre-group include deciding on a classroom space, time for the class, structure and flow, role of students, assessment, frequency of meetings, and how to use a virtual space. As mentioned, other chapters provide deeper insight into those areas. These areas are considered a part of the pre-group.

Stages of Group in Group Supervision

Stage 1: Forming

Forming is about setting the stage, laying the groundwork for the foundation of the group supervision course, and attempting to get everyone on the same page. Some of this work was already completed: CACREP standards, assignments and assessments, day and time, duration, and space to meet. We have already given emphasis to the faculty having a guiding goal in mind. A step that is often missed is giving a student agency to dictate how they want the group to run or to name their expectations. A well-established group will have identified rules and individual and group goals. This should be broached in the first session and ideally finished formulating by the third session. This is not to say things can't change during a 15–17-week course, but by week three, much of the foundation should be settled.

Rules are crucial to have established a well-functioning group. Some rules will have been pre-identified because of the academic setting. Students typically have a maximum number of class sessions they can miss (if any) and attendance, therefore, is expected. The group is a closed group because students must register for a section. Assignments will have been determined in advance and students will know how many case presentations, video demonstrations, and papers will be expected to be delivered and complete. Rules that need to be established with the group will be about participation (how often and what it looks like), expectations for giving feedback to group members, how to give critical feedback, and how to work through challenging moments when critical feedback is provided. Faculty strive toward gaining consensus and must keep in mind giving members the agency to develop these norms and rule collectively. Having a collective voice in forming the foundation for the group will lead toward better group cohesion and functioning.

Stage 2: Storming

Bernard and Goodyear (2019) discuss the storming stage as a time in which members are working through power struggles and dealing with between-member competitiveness. The competition can be coupled with other cognitions and considerations of vulnerability, insecurity, anxiousness, desire to be liked, and wanting to fit in. Simply put, no one wants to look incompetent or dumb in front of their peers. Additionally, help seeking behaviors may be lacking and prevent members from opening up or sharing their struggles for similar perceived threats of looking incompetent in front of their peers or in the eyes of the evaluating faculty. Competition may in fact be less about wanting to be better than everyone else and may be more about not wanting to appear less than everyone else.

Faculty work toward shifting the competitive environment toward one that allows members to feel safe for working through their struggles outwardly. The goal in storming is to move members past being performative, passive, and parroting, toward authentic and genuine engagement. To get members to that point, the faculty needs to foster elements of trust and support so that members believe they will be met with empathy, compassion, and encouragement when they are vulnerable and seek help. Members need to experience these elements to help them shed the fear of judgment or being rebuked.

This process can be a bit of an anomaly because the strongest support of the endeavor is when a student models the desired behaviors for their peers. Relying on a member to do that in the face of the perceived threats is a bit like waiting for a bird to land on your hand. Faculty may have some success in moving students through the storming by modeling with their own vulnerability about the struggles they have had in their clinical work. Other options include:

1. Using case studies from previous students to highlight areas they struggled in, the help they needed, and feedback they received from the group. This can normalize what students are feeling in a way that breaks the ice without putting the spotlight on the student.
2. Role playing giving feedback using pre-scripted case consultations. Students can act as if they were the intern in that situation and other members can practice giving critical feedback.
3. Rapport building activities and ice breaker exercises. Leaning into group theory, members who feel a closer connection with each other are more likely to engage authentically with vulnerability. To get members connected, faculty can use any kind of activity or icebreaker that allows members to get to know each other (outside of academic

content) on varying personal levels. This will also aid in building a trusting environment and increasing synergy among group members. This will move members away from feeling like they are unable to relate to their peers and increase awareness of how they are, usually, more similar than they are not.

4. Ongoing assessment of group dynamics. Corey and colleagues (2015) in their book *Group Techniques* provide insight into steps to take for preparing members for a group and information on what is happening interpersonally with members that interfere with their participation and connection. Readers are encouraged to do more reading on leading groups to gain insight into areas that they can consider and assess within their own groups as it relates to building cohesion and navigating storming.

Stage 3: Norming

How is norming different from the forming? Consider the forming to be the "what" and the norming to be the "how." In storming the faculty works through nuances that prevent getting to norming and later performing. Norms can be explicitly created and connected to the established rules. Norms may also happen organically. Faculty should carefully monitor and address group dynamics that contribute to the development of maladaptive norms. For instance, if it becomes customary for one individual to consistently participate first and dominate feedback or discussion, such a norm may discourage other members from taking initiative in leadership or active engagement. Remember that members will avoid participating for fear of looking less than their peers. If they know one person will always lead the charge, it gives them a pass to not participate.

Another dynamic to be attending to is collusion. Cliques, pre-existing friendships, and even romantic relationships are common in university supervision groups. Collusion, although not uncommon, is not a positive group dynamic. Collusion causes separation, further competition, be a threat, and corrode group cohesion (Jacobs et al., 2022). These are just two examples of group dynamics that foster maladaptive norming. A faculty can be directive in establishing norms to prevent maladaptive group dynamics from dictating norms. Possible approaches include:

1. Setting a schedule for each supervision session that is the same routine every session. Predictable frameworks prevent members from steering it in unhelpful or unproductive directions. The schedule should be time certain, and faculty must stick to the time frames. This establishes the norm for routine.

2. Ice breakers and activities that require members to co-mingle with different members each time. This sets a norm that members cannot stay in the same cliques or groups every time. It will prevent collusion from evolving and interfering with group processes.

3. A different student to present case studies, video demonstration, or consultation each week. While this may be standard practice, faculty still need to be mindful about how they intentionally engage different members equally throughout the supervision course. This establishes the norm that everyone will participate in consultation and feedback.

4. Using group approaches that require everyone to participate. Rounding is a simple method to make sure everyone provides feedback before moving on. Faculty have different options for who they start with, the order they go in, and how long or what each person says. This establishes the norm that everyone will participate, and the same person will not dominate the sharing process. When members know what is expected of them to share, they are more likely to engage meaningfully and not be inhibited by perceived threats.

5. Using group leadership skills, as detailed in Jacobs et al. (2022) to steer the group process. This can include calling on members who are silent, cutting off dominating members, moving members into different small groups or spots in the room, confronting disruptive group dynamics, and developing rules or norms on the spot. The faculty is also the group leader. At times they are more assertive in guiding students in the norming process and maintaining their position of authority. Failure to attend to group dynamics, being passive about problematic dynamics, and not taking control of the tone of the group will lead to unproductive and ineffective supervision groups. This will negatively impact self-efficacy and professional development in students. At times a faculty may need to intervene at a higher level, we discuss this in the chapters on assessment and legal and ethical issues.

Stage 4: Performing

Getting to the performing stage is a primary goal for the group process. In an academic course that is a minimum of eight weeks up toward 15–18 weeks, a faculty might aim to reach this stage halfway through the term. To reach this stage, is to be attentive and intentional in the first three stages because there is no guarantee that by midterm you will be performing. Additionally, the stages are fluid. At any time, a disruption may occur, and the group can return to storming and norming. This may be due to several reasons such as a member leaving or being terminated from the program, difficult interpersonal relationships, challenging feedback, or outside situations interfering with a member's ability to engage with the group in the present manner. Faculty leaders are never done attending to group dynamics or the group process, even when they feel that their supervision group has reached this stage. Potential signs, but not all inclusively, of being in the working stage include:

1. Members taking initiative and leadership independently
2. Quiet members speaking up more
3. Members working intentionally with each other
4. Depth and quality of feedback and consultation
5. Challenging or confronting appropriately
6. Working being done in a highly proficient manner
7. Evaluation reports from site supervisors
8. Positive assessment outcomes
9. Acquisition of counseling skills, increased self-awareness, and competencies

Not all groups reach this stage. At times variance that is outside of a faculty's control interferes with moving through storming and norming. Also, there can periods where the group stagnates. A faculty may consider changing the layout of the group to move through the stagnation. Lastly, as we discussed that everyone is unique and the group will potentially have more heterogenous factors than homogenous, some members may not move past their fears and insecurities to allow them to engage in the group process at the desired level. Given that the group is time certain and will end, some members may need more time before getting through their own storming to reach norming. This can cause a group to not fully move together with the cohesion and synergy desired for effective progression through the stages. Albeit these considerations, a faculty still strives for fidelity in their group leadership and attending to the dynamics throughout the stages.

Stage 5: Adjourning

The adjourning stage will happen no matter where the group is at in their process. Faculty plan for this stage by considering what academic components will happen at the end. Faculty should avoid adding new elements that will bring up new pieces to attend to, due to not having time to properly address them. In the adjourning stage a group leader considers unfinished business, reflecting on the group for what members have learned, helping members address what still needs to be worked on, and planning for the next phase of their journey.

For practicum students, faculty consider that phase one of fieldwork is completed, and students are heading into the more intensive component of the fieldwork journey. If a faculty member continues working with the group, the adjourning is more of a pause before continuing the group supervision work. The same method for infusing group theory into group supervision will be applied and the group may continue on in the performing stage, if they were previously in that stage. If they are not in the performing stage, the faculty will continue working with the group to move them to that stage. There is no legitimate need to start the process over if one is continuing with the same group from practicum to internship. Rather a faculty is cognizant of where the group was at when they ended and continues to work with a potential new goal in mind that is reflective of the internship needs and will allow the group to keep moving forward with cohesion and a productive group process.

If there are two sections of internship to facilitate completing the required 600 hours, and the group is moving from internship 1 to internship 2, the mindset of continuation of the group process with similar procedures will be maintained. For students completing fieldwork phase and moving onto the next step in their professional career, faculty can consider discussion related to pursuing licensure, maintaining liability insurance, continued group supervision opportunities, and aiding students in developing personal growth plans to follow post-graduation.

If the faculty is not continuing to supervise the group and a new faculty member is taking over the group, there are different considerations to address. Within group theory is the imperativeness of the leader building strong relationships with members and facilitating an environment in which the members trust the leader and members can operate within appropriate power dynamics with the leader. Additionally, the leader strives to foster cohesion that allows members to also take leadership within the group. These dynamics are reinforced within the rules and norms. A new university supervisor, working with an established group, is essentially starting over in the process of building trust, cohesion, rapport, and power dynamics. The barrier may be that the group will be resistant to the process because of the norms and cohesion previously built with a different faculty, especially if the leadership style of the new faculty is different than the previous faculty. Although the new faculty is starting over, the attending work will be largely the same with identifying the group process factors that are impeding cohesion and rapport building, establishing rules, leading the group through storming toward norming, and striving for the performance stage. Procedurally, the new faculty will proceed with designing, organizing, and facilitating the academic components.

Group Process and Dynamics

With group procedure being adequately discussed, the next areas to understand are group process and dynamics. As a faculty considers what to do procedurally in each stage, attention to process included ongoing assessment of cohesion, relationships, trust, norms, cross cultural issues, and supervisory tasks of giving and receiving feedback (Riva & Cornish, 1995). While the theoretical frameworks of group counseling and models of group supervision highlight the imperatives for attending to group process, researchers note that supervisors pay less attention to process than they have historically (Riva & Cornish, 2008). This may be due to the high demands of procedural tasks that supervisors (including faculty) have to attend to during the limited amount of time required by accreditation for supervision.

Group dynamics are made up of the intrapersonal and interpersonal factors and affect the group process. As discussed, group procedures need to consider these factors because they can either support or impede the process from moving forward in the described model. These factors can include developmental levels of students, emotional maturity and intelligence, multicultural and diversity, level of readiness, mental health considerations, and invisible diversity elements such as neurodiversity and physical ability. Specifically, Hoffman and colleagues (2005) note that the content of feedback, openness of supervisees, supervisory relationship, and other mentioned contextual issues will either facilitate or hinder supervision depending on the supervisor's skill level in facilitation. Additionally, Bogo and colleagues (2007) discussed that the supervision students' perception of their supervisor's competence, management of power dynamics, evaluation role, and intervention choices play a large role in the group process. Therefore, supervisors need to consider what their training needs are in facilitating supervision groups given the complex and variety of dynamics that need to be attended to, to support positive group process and still be able to attend to the procedures.

While emphasis in training is not intentionally placed on group topics, the discussion in the research literature on group processes in supervision is over 20 years old. Tebb and colleagues (1996) discussed that supervisors have insufficient skills to manage the complexities of groups they tend to resort to unhelpful or irrelevant practices, such as unnecessary storytelling, that cause the negative group process to become stressful and intense. Specific dynamics that require facilitators to be skilled in group facilitation include student anxiety, perceived negative affects, personality differences, cultural identity, fear of embarrassment, sexual attraction, and significant mental health issues (Ellis & Douce, 1994; Enyedy et al., 2003). While making mistakes are something students actively avoid and anxiety can undermine the fostering of group process, both anxiety and mistakes are necessary conditions for individual's acquisition of learning and the development growth of group process (Christensen & Kline, 2001).

Given the necessity of these factors, the need for skilled leadership is high because there are still significant risks involved. Negative feedback or a lack of constructive feedback given equitably among students can inhibit sharing and increase anxiety and shame among members. These problems in the feedback process cause issues in the supervisory relationship and group cohesion. When not properly addressed, the group process and opportunity for learning is negatively, sometimes severely, impacted (Linton & Hedstrom, 2006).

Strategies for University Supervisors to Attend to Negative Group Dynamics: Research-Informed Approaches

University supervisors play a pivotal role in shaping the effectiveness of group supervision. When negative group dynamics—such as resistance, conflict, anxiety, disengagement, or breakdowns in trust—emerge, supervisors must respond with evidence-based strategies and intentionality. Recent literature discusses the importance of proactive, relationally attuned interventions to foster productive group climates (Borders et al., 2020; Bernard & Goodyear, 2019).

Proactive Assessment and Observation

Supervisors should consistently assess the group climate, watching for signs of withdrawal, persistent conflict, or uneven participation. Structured check-ins, direct observation, and regular feedback are recommended strategies for surfacing unspoken concerns (Ladany et al., 2021).

Establish Clear Norms and Expectations

Clearly articulated norms around respect, confidentiality, and feedback help set the tone for psychological safety. Research highlights the value of collaboratively developed group agreements to promote shared responsibility (Okech & Rubel, 2018).

Foster Open Communication

Cultivating a culture of honest and respectful dialogue is essential. Supervisors can model transparency and invite members to discuss challenges and conflicts openly, thus reducing defensiveness and building trust (Trepal et al., 2019).

Address Power Dynamics and Inclusivity

Contemporary studies emphasize the necessity of attending to cultural, neurodiverse, and intersectional identities within groups. Supervisors should intentionally foster inclusivity and be mindful of their own authority to ensure equitable participation (Hernandez et al., 2020; Singh et al., 2020).

Utilize Targeted Interventions

When negative dynamics surface, literature supports the use of structured feedback exercises, conflict resolution strategies, and tailored interventions (Borders et al., 2020). These approaches help reframe issues and promote empathy and understanding.

Encourage Constructive Feedback and Growth Mindset

Modeling effective feedback and normalizing mistakes as part of the learning process reduces shame and fosters a growth mindset in supervisees (Borders et al., 2020; Ladany et al., 2021).

Attend to Emotional and Psychological Safety

This research reinforces the importance of emotional attunement by supervisors, who must intervene when anxiety, embarrassment, or distress threatens group cohesion. Creating space for emotional processing is linked with positive group outcomes (Trepal et al., 2019; Okech & Rubel, 2018).

Seek Consultation and Supervision

Supervisors are encouraged to pursue their own ongoing consultation and reflective supervision to address complex or entrenched group issues (Borders et al., 2020; Bernard & Goodyear, 2019).

By integrating these research-supported strategies, university supervisors can mitigate negative group dynamics and foster learning environments that promote professional growth and collaborative relationships. Attending to group process as well as procedural concerns leads to more transformative outcomes for both students and supervisors.

Table 7.1 provides a chart highlighting procedures and process for university supervisors to consider. Supervisors should integrate these principles to foster collaborative, productive, and supportive group supervision settings that promote professional growth for all participants.

TABLE 7.1 Research-Informed Guide to Fostering Transformative Group Supervision

Domain	Action/Strategy	Best Practices	Research Reference
Inclusivity & Identity	Attend to cultural, neurodiverse, and intersectional identities	Intentionally foster inclusivity; be mindful of authority and power dynamics; ensure equitable participation	Hernandez et al. (2020), Singh et al. (2020)
Targeted Interventions	Address negative dynamics	Use structured feedback, conflict resolution, and tailored interventions to promote empathy and understanding	Borders et al. (2020)
Feedback and Growth Mindset	Model effective feedback	Normalize mistakes; reduce shame; foster growth mindset in supervisees	Borders et al. (2020), Ladany et al. (2021)
Emotional and Psychological Safety	Monitor emotional climate	Intervene when anxiety or distress arises; create space for emotional processing to support group cohesion	Trepal et al. (2019), Okech and Rubel (2018)
Consultation and Reflective Supervision	Seek ongoing support	Pursue consultation and reflective supervision to address complex group issues	Borders et al. (2020), Bernard and Goodyear (2019)
Group Process Awareness	Monitor interactions and procedures	Attend to both group process and procedural concerns; recognize complex dynamics to ensure effective supervision	Corey et al. (2015), Holloway and Johnston (1985)
Emphasizing Group Dynamics	Highlight importance of group dynamics	Failure to attend to dynamics may compromise learning and development; supervision must recognize and address variety of group phenomena	Bogo et al. (2007), Ellis and Douce (1994), Enyedy et al. (2003)

Conclusion

Effective group supervision in counseling hinges on reflective consultation, vigilant awareness of group processes, and an intentional focus on group dynamics. Supervisors are encouraged to seek ongoing consultation and engage in reflective practices to navigate complex group issues, as these challenges require attentiveness to the subtle interplay of interactions and procedural concerns. Recognizing and addressing intricate group dynamics is essential, as neglecting these phenomena can undermine both supervisee development and group learning. Drawing on the literature, these practices ensure that group supervision remains responsive, developmentally attuned, and capable of fostering a transformative learning environment.

References

Bernard, J. M., & Goodyear, R. K. (2019). *Fundamentals of clinical supervision* (6th ed.). Boston, MA: Pearson.

Bogo, M., Regehr, C., Power, R., & Regehr, G. (2007). When values collide: Field instructors' experiences of providing feedback and evaluating competence. *The Clinical Supervisor, 26*(1/2), 99–117.

Borders, L. D., Glosoff, H. L., Welfare, L. E., Hays, D. G., DeKruyf, L., & Perrone-McGovern, K. (2020). Best practices in clinical supervision in counseling and psychotherapy. *Journal of Counseling & Development, 98*(3), 316–327.

Council for Accreditation of Counseling and Related Educational Programs (CACREP). (2024). *2024 Standards.* Retrieved from https://www.cacrep.org/for-programs/2024-cacrep-standards/

Christensen, T. M., & Kline, W. B. (2001). A qualitative investigation of the group supervision experience. *Journal for Specialists in Group Work, 26*(1), 81–99.

Corey, G. Corey, M. S., Callanan, P., & Russel, J. M. (2015). *Group techniques* (4th ed.). Stamford, CT: Cengage Learning.

Ellis, M. V., & Douce, L. A. (1994). Group supervision of novice clinical supervisors: Eight recurring issues. *Journal of Counseling & Development, 72,* 520–525.

Enyedy, K. C., Arcinue, F., Puri, N. N., Carter, J. W., Goodyear, R. K., & Getzelman, M. A. (2003). Hindering phenomena in group supervision: Implications for practice. *Professional Psychology: Research and Practice, 34,* 312–317.

Hoffman, M. A., Hill, C. E., Holmes, S. E., & Freitas, G. F. (2005). Supervisor perspective on the process and outcome of giving easy, difficult, or no feedback to supervisees. *Journal of Counseling Psychology, 52,* 3–13.

Holloway, E. L., & Johnston, R. (1985). Group supervision: Widely practiced but poorly understood. *Counselor Education and Supervision, 24*(4), 332–340.

Hernandez, P., Garcia, M., & Hunter, L. (2020). Culturally responsive supervision in counseling. *Journal of Counselor Leadership and Advocacy, 7*(1), 24–36.

Jacobs, E., Schimmel, C. J., Masson, B., & Harvill, R. (2022). *Group counseling: Strategies and skills* (9th ed.). Solana Beach, CA: Cognella.

Ladany, N., Walker, J. A., & Melincoff, D. S. (2021). Supervision in counseling: Recent advances and future directions. *The Counseling Psychologist, 49*(1), 7–32.

Linton, J. M., & Hedstrom, S. M. (2006). An exploratory qualitative investigation of group processes in group supervision: Perceptions of masters-level practicum students. *The Journal for Specialists in Group Work, 31,* 51–72.

Okech, J. E., & Rubel, D. (2018). *Group counseling: Strategies and skills* (9th ed.). Boston, MA: Cengage Learning.

Riva, M. T., & Cornish, J. A. E. (1995). Group supervision practices at psychology predoctoral internship programs: A national survey. *Professional Psychology: Research and Practice, 26,* 523–525.

Riva, M. T., & Cornish, J. A. E. (2008). Group supervision practices at psychology predoctoral internship programs: 15 years later. *Training and Education in Professional Psychology, 2,* 18–25.

Singh, A. A., Gonzalez, M., & Giordano, A. (2020). Social justice and group supervision: Best practices. *Journal for Specialists in Group Work, 45*(2), 97–110.

Tebb, S., Manning, D. W., & Klaumann, T. K. (1996). A renaissance of group supervision in practicum. *The Clinical Supervisor, 14*(2), 39–51.

Trepal, H. C., Bailie, J., & Leeth, C. (2019). The role of emotional processing in group supervision. *The Clinical Supervisor, 38*(1), 50–67.

Tuckman, B. W., & Jensen, M. A. C. (1977). Stages of small group development revisited. *Group & Organizational Studies, 2,* 419–427.

CHAPTER 8
CULTURALLY RESPONSIVE UNIVERSITY SUPERVISION IN COUNSELING FIELDWORK

Abstract

Culturally responsive supervision is paramount to effective counselor preparation programs. Bernard and Goodyear (2019) espouse that the best supervision practices foster their relationship with the supervisee's, centered on cultural humility, ongoing self-awareness, and openness to learning from supervisee's diverse backgrounds. As the makeup of the counseling profession continues to diversify, counselor educators and supervisors must be proficient in their cultural responsivity when working across cultural boundaries. Sue and colleagues encourage supervisors to engage in ongoing self-reflection to acknowledge their biases and privileges, as well as to actively integrate multicultural perspectives into supervision practices. Therefore, culturally responsive supervision moves beyond conventional guidance and aims to create a learning environment where diversity, equity, and inclusion are pillar to the personal and professional growth of interns. This chapter will identify the holistic process as well as identify models for use.

Culturally Responsive Supervision

Culturally responsive supervision, by university supervisors, refers to the active integration of a philosophy and subsequent mindset that acknowledges and includes interns' cultural identities, lived experiences, and worldviews into the supervisory process. Professional codes in counseling explicitly call for multicultural competence which makes culturally responsive supervision an ethical duty. Culture is not an adjacent concern but rather the heart of the teaching-learning relationship. The supervisor is a cultural navigator who facilitates discussions, explorations, and processes that are culturally inclusive, honor differences, and promote critical self-reflection.

DOI: 10.4324/9781003356776-9

Supervisors begin by nurturing cultural awareness, acknowledging both their own backgrounds and biases as well as those of their students and clients (Sue et al., 1992). This process is rooted in cultural humility, fostering openness and a genuine willingness to learn from others rather than adopting a stance of expertise over different cultures (Hook et al., 2013). Supervision in fieldwork courses should consider the cultural, social, and institutional factors that influence each student's experience, following the principle of contextual relevance (Stoltenberg et al., 1998). Through critical reflection, supervisors and interns engage in ongoing self-examination of their values, assumptions, and beliefs—a process essential for ethical practice (Falender & Shafranske, 2007). The goal is to empower by amplifying the voices and agency of students from historically marginalized groups.

Culturally responsive supervision involves overseeing both the intern and the clients they serve. Interns who receive culturally responsive supervision are more likely to enhance their self-efficacy, leading them toward growth and effective counseling skills. By honoring the lived realities and voices of each intern, supervisors create a collaborative journey marked by mutual respect and curiosity. This dynamic process encourages intentional dialogue around power, privilege, and difference, fostering a space where interns feel valued and equipped to navigate complex cultural contexts in their professional roles. The supervision work can empower interns to approach their own practice with the same commitment to equity and critical self-inquiry. Interns who are culturally attuned are more likely to build therapeutic relationship with clients that built upon trust and rapport, which can lead to successful outcomes in counseling.

The supervisory work also includes working with site supervisors and supporting interns. Not every field supervisor will be at a level of knowledge, awareness, or competence that each diverse intern will ideally benefit from. Additionally, not every site supervisor takes initiative to engage in dialogues regarding diversity with their intern; although researchers have found this to be a critically significant experience for the intern (White-Davis et al., 2016). Having a safe and trusting relationship with a site supervisor is a significant factor when considering if the internship experience is going to positively impact the intern (Wong et al., 2013). Internship students do not always feel confident or safe to confront or engage in difficult dialogues with their site supervisors. Thus, it is the job of the university supervisor to either mediate, mitigate, inform, educate, or intervene with the site supervisor when opportunities arise in which the intern needs support. Also, the university supervisor should consider, preemptively, how they can support, educate, and increase awareness on diversity topics for site supervisors.

Models of Culturally Responsive Supervision

Several models have been developed to guide supervisors in fostering cultural responsiveness within the supervisory relationship.

Multicultural Supervision Model

Sue et al. (1992) laid the groundwork for multicultural competency, emphasizing the supervisor's awareness, knowledge, and skills concerning cultural issues. Supervisors are encouraged to recognize their own cultural perspectives, understand the cultural worldviews of supervisees, and develop interventions that are culturally relevant (Sue et al., 1992).

The Discrimination Model

Bernard's Discrimination Model (Bernard, 1979) is widely used for clinical supervision and can be adapted for multicultural contexts. This model encourages supervisors to flexibly shift roles—as teacher, counselor, and consultant—while considering the supervisee's cultural background and the unique power dynamics present (Bernard & Goodyear, 2019).

The Integrated Developmental Model (IDM)

The IDM (Stoltenberg & Delworth, 1987; Stoltenberg et al., 1998) considers supervisees' developmental stages and incorporates cultural responsiveness by tailoring supervision to the evolving cultural awareness and competence of each trainee.

The Critical Events Model

Ladany, Friedlander, and Nelson (2005) proposed that supervision should focus on addressing culturally significant "critical events"—moments when cultural identities, differences, or misunderstandings emerge. Supervisors can use these opportunities for in-depth reflection and growth (Ladany et al., 2005).

The Intersectionality Framework

This approach, articulated by scholars such as Collins and Bilge (2016), recognizes that individuals hold multiple, intersecting identities (e.g., race, gender, class, ability) that shape their experiences in complex ways. Culturally responsive supervision using this framework attends to how intersecting identities impact both supervisee and client experiences (Collins & Bilge, 2016).

The Target Model for Social Justice Supervision

The model created by Ellison and colleagues (2024) utilizes roles from the *Discrimination Model* (Bernard, 1979) to centralize behaviors of self-awareness, focus on worldviews and the supervisory relationship, employ social justice interventions, and evaluated the effectiveness of the supervision work. The model is holistic and works with all relevant stakeholders in an intern's system.

Social Justice Supervision Model

The proposed model Dollarhide, Hale, and Stone-Sabali (2021) developed for social justice supervision integrates multicultural and social justice principles into counseling relationships, emphasizing intersectionality, systemic oppression, and empowerment. Drawing from the MSJCC framework, it redefines supervisory goals to prioritize cultural affirmation and liberation, utilizing systemic and post structural perspectives, power analysis, mutual learning, and identity development. The model follows four stages: supervisor self-evaluation, supervisee identity exploration, teaching social justice systems, and collaborative processing of social justice work. Throughout these stages, cultural humility, critical consciousness, and reflective practices are emphasized to disrupt hegemonic discourses, share power, and foster culturally responsive interventions.

Strategies for Culturally Responsive Supervision

The internship and fieldwork experiences can build and boost an intern's self-efficacy and competence. That self-efficacy and competence, in turn, can aid in obtaining successful client outcomes for the counseling intern. These aspects are imperative for an intern as they are about to emerge into the field in order that begin their professional career with self-assurance in their abilities, professional identity, and value their skill sets.

Supportive supervision and supervisory practices are critical for the enhancement of the aforementioned constructs (White-Davis et al., 2016). Students of color frequently experience supervision that is not culturally responsive and as a consequence suffer both professionally and personally (Burkhard et al., 2006). Therefore, implementing culturally responsive supervision requires intentionality and creativity. Supervisors must move beyond "one size fits all" models, embracing practices that are flexible and adaptive (Bernard & Goodyear, 2019; Sue et al., 1992).

We suggest the following steps, gleaned from research, for university supervisors to follow. This list is not exhaustive, and any supervisor must stay engaged in continuing education especially as the research and makeup of counselors continues to grow.

Begin with Self-awareness

Supervisors must begin with an honest appraisal of their own cultural identities, biases, and blind spots. Continuing education on multicultural issues, experiences of interns in counseling programs, and effective cross-cultural supervisors' practices is imperative. Supervisors should seek opportunities to gain feedback on their practices with a stance of humility and commitment to growth (Collins & Bilge, 2016; Falender & Shafranske, 2007). Assessment of cultural competence for coordinators, university, and site supervisors is an important aspect of self-awareness work. Self-assessment inventories, reflective journals, observed supervisor sessions, and feedback from stakeholders with allowing one to gauge where they are in their development and identify areas for growth (Falender & Shafranske, 2007).

Creating a Safe and Inclusive Environment

Supervisors are responsible for creating a climate and promoting a program culture where students feel included and valued. The climate includes the supervision classroom space, online platforms, relevant handbooks and materials, and the site in which interns are placed. Therefore, coordinators and university supervisors must see the whole picture and not just one part of the climate. University supervisors need to be aware of the visible and invisible diversity elements of students and site supervisors. In the construction of a safe inclusive environment, all materials, aspects, and approaches should include inclusive language, access to equitable resources, translated materials, and identified support systems as appropriate.

The goal is to decrease fear, shame, and anxiety experienced by cross-cultural individuals that prevent their abilities to access services by normalizing inclusion and potential needs. In the supervision space, university supervisors can explicitly address issues of power, privilege, disenfranchisement, discrimination, bias, and racism to model the types of dialogues they expect to see in case consultation, mentoring, role-modeling, and skill building work (Ladany et al., 2005; Constantine & Sue, 2007). These conversations need to extend into the work done with site-supervisors. Orientation and training provided to site supervisors must contain cultural competence building, education on culturally responsive supervision practices, and methods for assessing cultural competence to identify subsequent training needs. Ultimately, coordinators and university supervisors want to create an environment in which interns will feel safe to speak up when issues arise.

Utilizing supervision models can be advantageous for creating safe and supportive environments. Supervision models should be flexible, allowing for the incorporation of students' languages, cultural traditions, and community resources. For example, using narrative supervision strategies (Morgan, 2000) can empower supervisees to share their stories and reflect on cultural influences in their practice. Additionally, supervisors are advised to collaborate with culturally diverse mentors and consult with experts when addressing unfamiliar cultural dilemmas. Finally, research points to the importance of outcome evaluation: supervisors should solicit feedback about the supervision process and supervisee satisfaction with the cultural responsiveness of their training (Inman, 2006). By embedding these evidence-based strategies, universities can ensure that their supervision practices meet the evolving needs of a diverse student body and prepare future counselors to work competently and compassionately across cultures.

Integrating Multicultural Content and Promoting Critical Dialogue

Internship classes should intentionally weave multicultural theory, research, and case examples into the curriculum. Supervisors can encourage students to explore how cultural variables—such as race, ethnicity, gender, sexual orientation, religion, ability status, and socioeconomic background—shape counseling processes (Sue et al., 1992; Collins & Arthur, 2010). Assignments should include prompts, areas to address, and accreditation standards that will allow interns to engage in cultural conversations to build a mindset in which culture is at the heart of the clinical lens, and not an ancillary item to address. Additionally, university supervisors must consider how they will broach the cross-cultural experiences interns are having, based on their cultural identity, in their internship experiences. In Table 8.1, we provide research backed practices for supervisors to adopt as they integrate multicultural competency building into their supervision work.

TABLE 8.1 Research Supportive Practices for University Supervisors

Practice	Description	Source
Model Vulnerability and Growth	Demonstrate willingness to make mistakes, apologize, and learn alongside supervisees	Ladany et al. (2005)
Solicit Feedback	Routinely gather anonymous feedback from students regarding the inclusivity and effectiveness of supervision	Vasquez et al. (2008)
Adapt to Context	Flexibly tailor supervision to the specific needs, backgrounds, and goals of each intern and site placement	Stoltenberg et al. (1998)
Commit to Lifelong Learning	Stay current with research, training, and literature in multicultural counseling and supervision	Sue et al. (1992)
Seek Support and Collaboration	Connect with colleagues, diversity offices, and professional organizations for resources and mentorship	Estrada et al. (2002)
Model Inclusive Dialogue	Address issues such as power, privilege, discrimination, and bias to normalize open, respectful discussion	Social Justice Supervision Models
Empower Advocacy and Allyship	Encourage supervisees to recognize and confront systemic barriers, fostering advocacy for equity and justice within their roles	Social Justice Supervision Models
Culturally Responsive Case Conceptualization	Integrate cultural, contextual, and societal factors into case discussions and supervision to deepen understanding and enhance interventions	Social Justice Supervision Models
Critical Self-reflection	Facilitate ongoing reflection about personal biases, positionality, and the impact of social structures in supervision and practice	Social Justice Supervision Models
Community Engagement	Promote involvement with community partners and organizations, prioritizing collaboration with those who are impacted by inequities	Social Justice Supervision Models

Supervision should be a space not only for skill-building but for deep and meaningful conversations about cultural differences, systemic oppression, intersectionality, and social justice. Supervisors must be prepared to facilitate difficult dialogues and help interns process discomfort, defensiveness, or uncertainty not only for clients but for themselves (Collins & Bilge, 2016; Ladany et al., 2005). Lastly, Culturally responsive supervision includes preparing students to advocate for themselves and their clients within institutional and community contexts. Supervisors can guide students in identifying systems of oppression and exploring strategies for social change, whether through direct counseling, community engagement, or policy advocacy (Constantine & Sue, 2007; Collins & Arthur, 2010).

University Supervisors as Advocates for Interns

In advocating for culturally diverse interns, university supervisors play a pivotal role in bridging the gap between academic preparation and real-world professional practice (Stoltenberg et al., 1998). They begin by establishing open, collaborative lines of communication with site supervisors, ensuring that expectations around cultural responsiveness are mutual and explicit (Vasquez et al., 2008). Supervisors often provide orientation sessions for site supervisors, highlighting the importance of cultural humility, adaptation, and an awareness of systemic inequities that may affect interns' experiences (Ladany et al., 2005).

University supervisors advocate by sharing relevant information about interns' unique backgrounds, strengths, and needs—always with the intern's consent—so that site supervisors can tailor mentorship and support accordingly (Stoltenberg et al., 1998). They encourage site supervisors to actively engage in dialogue about diversity-related challenges, inviting them to co-create solutions that affirm the intern's identity and foster a supportive learning environment (Ladany et al., 2005). When concerns arise, university supervisors intervene promptly, facilitating conversations that address microaggressions, bias, or misunderstandings, and modeling advocacy and allyship in action (Vasquez et al., 2008).

Additionally, university supervisors encourage site supervisors to integrate culturally responsive practices into daily routines—such as inviting interns to share cultural perspectives within team meetings, adapting case assignments to reflect diverse communities, and supporting participation in culturally significant events (Vasquez et al., 2008). They may also provide resources, training, or consultation opportunities to site supervisors, strengthening collective capacity for cultural competence (Stoltenberg et al., 1998).

This advocacy is most effective when supervisors remain visible and accessible throughout the internship, conducting regular check-ins with both interns and site supervisors. By championing cultural responsiveness as a shared value and responsibility, university supervisors help ensure that site-based experiences are not only educationally rich but also affirming and equitable for all interns (Ladany et al., 2005). In Table 8.2, we provide strategies for supervisors to consider in their advocacy work.

TABLE 8.2 Behavioral Strategies for Coordinators and University Supervisors

Behavioral Strategy	Description
Model Inclusive Dialogue	Address issues such as power, privilege, discrimination, and bias to normalize open, respectful discussion.
Use Inclusive Materials and Language	Ensure all resources and communications reflect diverse identities and use affirming, inclusive language.
Adapt Supervision Models	Employ flexible models that integrate students' languages, traditions, and community resources.
Solicit and Incorporate Feedback	Gather and use feedback from interns to improve the cultural responsiveness and inclusivity of supervision.
Facilitate Critical Multicultural Conversations	Encourage open exploration of cultural variables and provide safe spaces for processing discomfort or uncertainty.
Provide Resources and Training	Offer continual training and resources to site supervisors to build cultural competence.
Advocate for Intern Identity and Needs	Share relevant background information (with consent) to tailor mentorship and support.
Promote Collaborative Problem-Solving	Invite interns and site supervisors to co-create solutions to diversity-related challenges.
Support Participation in Culturally Significant Events	Encourage interns to engage in events and activities celebrating their cultural identities.
Conduct Regular Check-Ins	Maintain open, visible communication with interns and site supervisors throughout the internship.
Facilitate Difficult Dialogues	Guide discussions about systemic oppression, intersectionality, and social justice supportively.
Encourage Self-advocacy and Client Advocacy	Help interns identify systems of oppression and strategize for social change within their communities.
Empower Storytelling	Use narrative supervision to encourage sharing of personal and cultural experiences.
Consult with Cultural Experts	Seek advice from culturally diverse mentors when facing unfamiliar cultural dilemmas.
Adapt Case Assignments	Assign cases that reflect diverse client populations and multicultural perspectives.

Multilingual Supervision

Multilingual supervision is the practice in which supervision recognizes linguistic diversity and utilizes inclusive practices in affirmation of the diverse language(s) (Fuertes & Brobst, 2002). Incorporating multilingual resources into supervision is another vital practice. By providing counseling literature, assessment tools, and case studies in students' preferred languages, supervisors foster a more inclusive and accessible learning environment (Tang & Grothus, 2023). Fuertes (2004) highlights that such resources facilitate learning and promote equity.

Language mapping and needs assessment are important elements in multilingual supervision. Coordinators and university supervisor can begin by identifying the languages spoken by students and clients, while also assessing their comfort levels with English and any additional languages (Fuertes & Brobst, 2002). This approach is supported by Lau and Ng (2014), who emphasize that a thorough language assessment can contribute significantly to successful multicultural supervision. Additionally, counseling programs can also invest in training to develop linguistic sensitivity. Understanding how language shapes meaning, power dynamics, and rapport is critical. Workshops on linguistic equity and practices using inclusive terminology are recommended by Constantine and Sue (2006), who stress the importance of linguistic competence in diverse supervisory settings.

Encouraging code-switching during supervision can also be beneficial. Validating and allowing the use of first languages, especially when discussing complex emotions or cultural narratives, helps deepen understanding and rapport. Research by Chen and Martin (2005) indicated that code-switching enhances communication and supports the development of a trusting supervisory relationship. When language barriers arise, engaging interpreters or cultural brokers can facilitate effective communication. It is important that these professionals uphold the autonomy and voice of the student or supervisee. Lee et al. (2010) explain that the involvement of trained interpreters is effective in maintaining supervisee empowerment within supervision sessions.

Mentorship and peer support networks play a significant role in supporting multilingual students. Connecting interns with mentors who share similar linguistic backgrounds can help them navigate language-related challenges in professional environments. Estrada et al. (2002)

demonstrate the value of culturally and linguistically matched mentorship in fostering support and guidance. Finally, providing opportunities for feedback across languages ensures that interns can communicate openly and honestly. Allowing feedback in the supervisee's preferred language removes barriers and increases engagement. Vasquez et al. (2008) note that accessible feedback mechanisms enhance the overall effectiveness of supervision.

Supporting Interns with Invisible Diversity

Diversity is multidimensional, with visible and invisible identities. Diversity can include race, ethnicity, gender identity, ability (physical, cognitive, language), mental health, socioeconomic status, family identity, and other non-traditional identity makeups. As well, diversity is intersectional, with the relevant systems in an intern's life impacting the makeup of each identity, with each identity having influence or impact on the other. Culturally responsive supervision strives to attend to, and honor, the seen and unseen diverse identities.

A starting point is to seek to understand the multidimensional identities of the interns. This can be collected via needs assessments, questionnaires, or through in vivo methods. Coordinators will consider placements and site supervisors that can provide the support and accommodation needed, as well as provide equitable experiences for fieldwork. Assistive technology, spatial accommodations, working hours that are responsive to needs, and training on diversity sensitive supervision are just a few suggestions to consider as coordinators work as advocates for their interns. University supervisors consider the invisible diversities and adapt their teaching and delivery methods, supervision styles, technology use, and communication methods to be responsive to the needs of interns (Holtzman, 2004). Additionally, coordinators and university supervisors can develop partnerships with accessibility resource centers at their institution to provide resources for interns who may qualify for accommodations through the institution. That serves as an important legal support for interns both at the institution and at their internship sites. Ultimately, the goal is for interns not to suffer in silence out of fear, shame, or insecurity and to receive the services that will allow them to grow and succeed during fieldwork (Beatty & Kirby, 2006).

Culturally Responsive Assessment

Culturally responsive assessment is a practice that recognizes, appreciates, and responds to cultural differences when evaluating counseling interns (Sue & Sue, 2016). Standard assessment instruments, although widely promoted in the field and in this book, are not free from cultural bias and often developed with Eurocentric assumptions. This trend has the tendency to misrepresent the skills and competencies of interns from diverse backgrounds (Ridley et al., 2001). Additionally, a supervisor's competence is a key mitigating factor in preventing bias from interfering with fair assessment practices (Falender & Shafranske, 2007). Given the lack of standardized multicultural instruments and tools for assessment of counseling skills, and potentially limited opportunities for placing interns in culturally reflective systems, supervisors at any level must stay engaged with ongoing competency building and employ reflective practices when utilizing standardized assessment procedures. Below we provide research supported ideas.

Utilization of Multicultural Rubrics

When possible, coordinators can develop and utilize rubrics that incorporate cultural awareness and humility. This practice will lead to more reliable evaluations of cross-cultural interns (Harris et al., 2022). Coordinators can work with cultural stakeholders in the development of rubrics and tool, as well as appraising current standardized assessments, to increase fairer and more accurate evaluations (Ibrahim & Thompson, 2023). Additionally, Swank et al. (2023) introduced the *Multicultural Counseling Self-Efficacy Scale-Revised*, which was validated with diverse student intern cohorts and shown to predict counseling outcomes across multiple cultural groups.

Training and Reflection

As mentioned throughout the chapter, ongoing training and continuing education are crucial. Supervisors who engaged in ongoing cultural competence training demonstrated increased awareness of bias and more equitable evaluation practices (Kim & Smith, 2022). Reflective practices include individual and collective approaches that support building awareness for bias and identifying barriers that prevent equitable evaluations (Nguyen & Patel, 2023). These behaviors decrease unfairness and inequity in assessment.

Process-Oriented Assessment

A process-oriented framework looks at growth over time and not sole based on standardized benchmarks. This approach fosters adaptability and openness to cultural learning (Parker & Lee, 2021). Supervisors look at the whole picture of growth and development, taking into account cultural covariates that impact the process. Additionally, interns should be encouraged to reflect on their own cultural competence, strengths, and areas for growth. Self-assessment in interns increases and engagement and enhanced reflective practice in multicultural contexts (Rodriguez & Chen, 2023).

Feedback from Multiple Perspectives

Gathering data from multiple sources has been shown to reduce evaluator bias and increase assessment validity (Gomez et al., 2022). Coordinators and university supervisors consider in advance relevant stakeholders—clients, peers, site supervisors, cultural agents—as they develop sequences and procedures for evaluation. This may include developing additional rubrics and assessment tools for collecting data. Important to note is the continued validity testing of any rubric or tool developed within a counseling program.

Challenges in Implementing Culturally Responsive Supervision

Despite its clear benefits, culturally responsive university supervision presents challenges (Bernard & Goodyear, 2019). Supervisors may face institutional constraints, lack of resources, resistance from students or faculty, or their own discomfort with multicultural issues (Constantine, 2007). Some students may feel threatened or overwhelmed by discussions of culture, privilege, or oppression (Sue et al., 2008). Institutional barriers arise when university systems lack policies, curriculum, or support for culturally responsive practices (Inman, 2006). Time constraints, large class sizes, and limited access to multicultural materials can impede implementation (Constantine, 2007). Additionally, not all supervisors receive adequate training in multicultural supervision (Bernard & Goodyear, 2019).

To work through these barriers, we recommend starting at the department and program levels. Faculty groups need to develop a salient and deliberate philosophy about the culture of their program to be culturally inclusive and responsive. Ideally the faculty will be unified in their approaches. All materials—handbooks, contracts, forms—need to contain supportive language and policies for culturally responsive work. Site supervisors need to be trained in the Multicultural competencies and Social Justice advocacy, as well as oriented in their expectations for culturally responsive supervision.

Students across all programs and classes need engaged learning and experiences to develop and enhance multicultural competencies. Assessment of competencies needs to be systematically done across the curriculum and include opportunities to feedback and support for students and interns. At the broader systemic level, programs can work with deans, provosts, presidents and/or other relevant leaders at their academic institutions, to educate them on accreditation standards, the imperative for inclusion of multicultural, social justice, and advocacy topics, and the role the administration plays in promoting these values at the institutional level.

Conclusion

This chapter covers the critical components and challenges of implementing culturally responsive supervision in multilingual and diverse university settings. It highlights the importance utilizing culturally responsive supervision methods to attend to the visible and invisible diversity needs of interns. Coordinators and university supervisor acts as advocates on behalf of interns with sites and site supervisors. Despite clear benefits, culturally responsive supervision faces obstacles including insufficient resources, institutional barriers, and gaps in supervisor training or faculty buy-in. We recommend systemic changes at departmental and administrative levels, including cohesive philosophies, curriculum reforms, and comprehensive faculty and site supervisor training, as essential steps to promote equity, inclusion, and the professional growth of all interns.

Bibliography

Beatty, J. E., & Kirby, S. L. (2006). Beyond the legal environment: How stigma influences invisible identity groups in the workplace. *Employee Responsibilities and Rights Journal, 18*(1), 29–44.

Bernard, J. M. (1979). Supervisor training: A discrimination model. *Counselor Education and Supervision, 19*(1), 60–68.

Bernard, J. M., & Goodyear, R. K. (2019). *Fundamentals of clinical supervision* (6th ed.). New York, NY: Pearson.

Burkhard A. W., Johnson, A. J., Madson, M. B., Pruitt, N., & Contreras-Tadych, D. A. (2006). Supervisor cultural responsiveness and unresponsiveness in cross cultural supervision. *Journal of Counseling Psychology, 53*(3), 288–301.

Chen, E. C., & Martin, R. (2005). Implementation of multilingual supervision. *The Clinical Supervisor, 24*(2), 123–140.

Collins, P. H., & Bilge, S. (2016). *Intersectionality*. Cambridge: Polity Press.

Collins, S., & Arthur, N. (2010). Culture-infused counselling: A model for developing multicultural competence. *Counselling Psychology Quarterly, 23*(2), 217–233.

Constantine, M. G. (2007). Multicultural competence in supervision. In D. B. Pope-Davis, H. L. K. Coleman, W. M. Liu, & R. L. Toporek (Eds.), *Handbook of multicultural competencies in counseling & psychology* (pp. 383–398). Thousand Oaks, CA: Sage Publications.

Constantine, M. G., & Sue, D. W. (2006). Factors contributing to multicultural supervision competence. *Journal of Multicultural Counseling and Development, 34*(4), 286–296.

Constantine, M. G., & Sue, D. W. (2007). Perceptions of racial microaggressions among black supervisees in cross-racial dyads. *Journal of Counseling Psychology, 54*(2), 142–153.

Dollarhide, C. T., Hale, S. C., & Stone-Sabali, S. (2021). A new model for social justice supervision. *Journal of Counseling and Development, 99*, 104–113.

Ellison, S. E., Tierney, P., & Taylor, M. (2024). A target model for social justice supervision. *Teaching and Supervision in Counseling, 6*(3), 1–14.

Estrada, A. U., Durlak, J. A., & Juarez, S. C. (2002). Mentoring and peer support in multicultural supervision. *Professional Psychology: Research and Practice, 33*(3), 330–336.

Falender, C. A., & Shafranske, E. P. (2007). Competence in competency-based supervision practice: Construct and application. *Professional Psychology: Research and Practice, 38*(3), 232–240.

Fuertes, J. N. (2004). Supervision in bilingual counseling: Service delivery, training, and research considerations. *Journal of Multicultural Counseling and Development, 32*, 84–94.

Fuertes, J. N., & Brobst, K. (2002). Multilingual resources in counseling supervision. *Journal of Counseling & Development, 80*(1), 81–87.

Gomez, R., Patel, R., & Swank, J. (2022). Multi-perspective evaluation in counselor training: Reducing bias through inclusive feedback. *Journal of Counselor Education, 43*(4), 201–218.

Harris, L. M., Nguyen, V., & Lee, S. (2022). Multicultural rubrics and reliable assessment: Innovations in counselor education. *International Journal of Multicultural Education, 24*(2), 155–170.

Holtzman, L. (2004). Mining the invisible: Teaching and learning media and diversity. *The American Behavioral Scientist, 48*(1), 108–118.

Hook, J. N., Davis, D. E., Owen, J., Worthington, E. L., & Utsey, S. O. (2013). Cultural humility: Measuring openness to culturally diverse clients. *Journal of Counseling Psychology, 60*(3), 353–366.

Ibrahim, S., & Thompson, P. (2023). Contextualized evaluation in counselor intern assessment. *Counseling Today, 12*(1), 60–76.

Inman, A. G. (2006). Supervisor multicultural competence and its impact on supervisee satisfaction. *Journal of Counseling Psychology, 53*(4), 396–406.

Kim, J., & Smith, B. (2022). Supervisor cultural competence training and equitable evaluation practices. *Clinical Supervisor, 41*(2), 95–112.

Ladany, N., Friedlander, M. L., & Nelson, M. L. (2005). *Critical events in psychotherapy supervision: An interpersonal approach.* Washington, DC: American Psychological Association.

Lau, J., & Ng, K.-M. (2014). Conceptualizing the counseling training environment using Bronfenbrenner's ecological theory. *International Journal for the Advancement of Counseling, 36,* 423–439.

Lau, M. Y., & Ng, K. M. (2014). Multicultural supervision: Language mapping and assessment. *International Journal for the Advancement of Counselling, 36*(4), 396–408.

Lee, A., Smith, B., & Patel, R. (2023). Integrating multicultural competence into counselor education: Effects on intern development. *Journal of Counseling Training, 45*(2), 134–148.

Lee, E., Ng, K. M., Leong, F. T. L., & Tan, S. Y. (2010). Cultural brokers and interpreters in multicultural supervision. *Supervision in Counseling and Psychotherapy, 48*(1), 100–112.

Morgan, A. (2000). Narrative approaches in supervision. In *Narrative therapy and practice.* Adelaide, Australia: Dulwich Centre Publications.

Nguyen, V., & Patel, R. (2023). Reflective practices for multicultural supervisors. *Journal of Counseling Supervision, 39*(3), 287–304.

Parker, D., & Lee, S. (2021). Process-oriented frameworks for intern development. *Journal of Counselor Preparation and Supervision, 15*(2), 78–92.

Ratts, M. J., Singh, A. A., Nassar-McMillan, S., Butler, S. K., & McCullough, J. R. (2016). Multicultural and social justice counseling competencies:

Guidelines for the counseling profession. *Journal of Multicultural Counseling & Development, 44*(1), 28–48.

Ridley, C. R., Mendoza, D. W., Kanitz, B. E., Anger, H. A., & Zenk, R. (2001). Cultural sensitivity in counselor assessment: Challenges and solutions. *Journal of Counseling Psychology, 48*(2), 125–137.

Rodriguez, M., & Chen, H. (2023). Structured self-assessment protocols in multicultural counseling internships. *International Journal of Counselor Education, 36*(3), 165–179.

Stoltenberg, C. D., & Delworth, U. (1987). *Supervising counselors and therapists: A developmental approach.* San Francisco, CA: Jossey-Bass.

Stoltenberg, C. D., McNeill, B. W., & Delworth, U. (1998). *IDM supervision: An integrated developmental model for supervising counselors and therapists* (2nd ed.). San Francisco, CA: Jossey-Bass.

Sue, D. W., Arredondo, P., & McDavis, R. J. (1992). Multicultural counseling competencies and standards: A call to the profession. *Journal of Counseling & Development, 70*(4), 477–486.

Sue, D. W., & Sue, D. (2008). *Counseling the culturally diverse: Theory and practice* (5th ed.). Hoboken, NJ: John Wiley & Sons.

Sue, D. W., & Sue, D. (2016). *Counseling the culturally diverse: Theory and practice* (7th ed.). Hoboken, NJ: John Wiley & Sons.

Swank, J., Patel, R., & Lee, S. (2023). The multicultural counseling self-efficacy scale-revised: Validation and predictive outcomes. *Journal of Multicultural Counseling and Development, 51*(1), 19–34.

Tang, H.-Y., & Grothus, T. (2023). Supervisor training needs to work with emerging multilingual supervisees. *International Journal for the Advancement of Counseling, 45*, 577–593.

Vasquez, M. J. T. et al. (2008). Feedback mechanisms in multicultural supervision. *Professional Psychology: Research and Practice, 39*(2), 192–198.

White-Davis, T., Stein, E., & Karasz, A. (2016). The elephant in the room: Dialogues about race within cross-cultural supervisory relationships. *The International Journal of Psychiatry in Medicine, 51*(4), 347–356.

Wong, L. C. J., Wong, P. T. P., & Ishiyama, F. I. (2013). What helps and what hinders in cross-cultural supervision: A critical incident study. *The Counseling Psychologist, 4*(1), 66–85.

CHAPTER 9
LEGAL AND ETHICAL ISSUES

Abstract

University supervisors are fundamental in the formation of interns in counseling programs. In addition to the academic and supervision tasks, this role requires addressing legal and ethical issues that arise during the fieldwork process. While university supervisors establish standards and rules in advance as they relate to confidentiality, mandated reporting, evaluation, and professional expectations, they also must develop procedures for gatekeeping and intervening when issues arise. This chapter will cover the unique landscape of legal and ethical issues as well as provide a framework for remediation.

Legal and Ethical Landscape in Counseling Training Programs

The legal and ethical landscape in counseling training programs is complex and unique. While counseling is governed by laws, regulations, and ethical codes, university supervision demands a specialized and intense focus to ensure that interns are adhering to the aforementioned rules and codes, and behaving in professional manners at their sites, in the classroom, and in their communities. The array of issues that can come up is endless. University supervisors, who are gatekeepers, must be mindful that they are determining readiness for the field not only for professional and clinical skills, but also for personal dispositions. This process is not always clear cut, and supervisors must use their discernment in subjective situations to determine if interns need remediation, time away from the program, or to be dismissed. Below, we provide context for core areas that university supervisors will address and monitor.

DOI: 10.4324/9781003356776-10

Core Legal Responsibilities

Mandated Reporting

University supervisors are responsible for the welfare of the clients that interns are working with. They must ensure interns are aware of their responsibilities for mandated reporting, as the university supervisor is liable for cases in which reporting is required. At times the university supervisors will collaborate with the site supervisor to ensure that procedures are properly followed. Coordinators can establish training requirements and schedule training to be provided to interns and site supervisors to ensure they have the proper knowledge for procedures and are up to date on state or county specific regulations and procedures. Potential issues arise when site supervisors do not follow procedures and protocols. University supervisors will determine how to support site supervisors and intervene as needed.

Confidentiality and Privacy

University supervisors will educate their interns on the policies and procedures as they relate to ethical codes, state statutes, institutional policies, and relevant internship site rules. Also, interns need training on adherence to privacy laws such as HIPPA and the best practices for ensuring security and safety when using technology and virtual counseling. While some internship sites provide training on these topics, we encourage coordinators to determine a process for interns to systematically receive training and to have access to materials that provide ongoing assistance to achieve compliance with policies and regulations.

Informed Consent

Informed consent is a required part of the counseling process. It may also look different across professional identities. University supervisors ensure that interns are knowledgeable of the required procedures within their professional identities, can develop necessary forms and documents, and follow their relevant code of ethics. This topic may be covered in other academic courses and can be extended into supervision courses to focus on explaining the nature, goals, risks, and limitations of counseling. While site supervisors are also responsible for ensuring interns follow the procedures that are site specific, we advocate for coordinators and university supervisors to develop education components within the supervision courses for students to engage with to enhance the developmental growth work.

Informed consent also regards supervision. In the counseling program fieldwork handbooks, a measure of informed consent, coordinators address a breadth of topics related to expectations, evaluation, remediation, and more. Just as an informed consent document in a counseling setting is a legally binding document, so is the signed fieldwork handbook. In addition to the handbook, coordinators can develop informed consent documents for site supervisors and interns. Bernard and Goodyear (2019) provide examples of supervision contracts that can be used. Rather than rely on a variety of documents that are, or are not, used by site supervisors, coordinators can provide a systematic and uniform approach for interns and site supervisors in informed consent-or supervision contracts that detail the expectations of all parties involved.

Core Ethical Responsibilities

Ethical Behavior

University supervisors are responsible for addressing and attending to the ethical behaviors of interns. The spectrum of topics includes communication, dress, punctuality, romantic and personal relationships, technology use, substance use, behavior in the community, professionalism in the workplace. The list can continue and because the spectrum is very broad, we strongly advocate for coordinators, in collaboration with counseling departments—and even site supervisors—to determine the required dispositions (CACREP, 2024) in advance and in consideration of relevant ethical codes. This information, as it is required to be placed in the fieldwork handbook, is the foundation for addressing misbehaviors and determining if remediation or dismissal is needed.

University supervisors have two identified responsibilities: teaching and modeling ethical behavior. Interns will have completed an ethics course prior to fieldwork, and they will benefit from continued training and engagement with ethical decision-making models, applying ethical codes to casework, and activities that have them consider ethical dilemmas. This will foster their development of a professional and ethical mindset in their professional work. Also, university supervisors must exemplify ethical and moral conduct in each aspect of their role. From dual relationships, communication, transparency, advocacy, evaluation and further on, their behaviors will set a standard for interns to emulate.

Dual Relationships

Interns may find themselves in a variety of dual relationships. At times they are inevitable, they can be complex, and they can interfere with the fieldwork process. There are a variety of dynamics that can arise: interning in systems they grew up in, working with family members, romantic relationships, working with or around familiars from their systems, interning at the workplace, rural dynamics, and furthermore. Given that these situations cannot always be avoided, interns need help understanding how to operate ethically, maintain appropriate boundaries, and how to advocate for themselves when needed. Coordinators may determine which types of dual relationships are allowed and which will not be permitted. The university supervisors can help interns navigate the nuances and be an advocate on behalf of the intern with site supervisors and within systems when complications arise that are outside of the scope of the intern to handle.

Cultural Competence

Cultural competence is not only a skill that is fostered but is also an element that university supervisors are ethically obligated to monitor. In upholding the ethical principle to "do no harm" (ACA Code of Ethics, 2014), university supervisors are liable for the cross cultural clinical and counseling behaviors, services, and interactions of their interns. University supervisors promote diversity, equity, inclusion, humility, and social justice advocacy in their supervision work. They need to be equipped and ready to address issues with competency and capacity displayed by interns.

Site and Site Supervisor

Both legal and ethical issues can arise with sites and site supervisors. Failure to uphold laws and statutes, insurance fraud or abuse, and malpractice are potential legal issues that can arise. Ethical issues can include inappropriate dual relationships, unethical behavior in and out of sessions and professional work settings, forging internship documents, lying about intern hour accruements, not providing the required supervision, harmful environments, toxic workplace relationships, hostile supervision styles and relationships, and failure to meet supervisory expectations. This list is not exhaustive, however.

University supervisors work to create safe and supportive academic environments to encourage interns to share their truths about their experiences.

It is normal for interns to avoid sharing their struggles due to fear of negative consequences. University supervisors should consider methods for using self-disclosure and transparency to alert interns of situations that are illegal or unethical. This may foster interns to feel safe to share.

When issues do arise, university supervisors must be proactive with documenting the situation and gathering data or evidence. From there we encourage using the ACA 2014 Code of *Ethical Decision-Making Model* to address the situation. Possible approaches can include meeting with the supervisor to address the issue and developing a plan moving forward for growth, change, and monitoring. In some situations, the university supervisor and coordinator may need to remove an intern from a site due to the severity of the issues at hand. Lastly, coordinators can consider adding content to the orientation and training they provide to site supervisors on ethical expectations for supervising interns.

Supervising Interns in University Counseling Centers

Training centers provide both doctoral and master's level interns opportunities to practice supervision and counseling skills during fieldwork. There are unique ethical challenges associated with training in university counseling centers related to intern's competence, dual relationships, and value conflicts. Doctoral interns who are acting in clinical supervisor or director roles in counseling centers are still developing in their competencies for supervision and counseling. Coordinators and university supervisors need to closely monitor doctoral interns to ensure competent supervision is being provided. We call this supervision of supervision.

Doctoral interns will need support for navigating legal and ethical issues, just as any site supervisor would need. Another issue that arises is dual relationships. These relationships can be between master's level students and university students, doctoral and master's students, and interns with other staff or faculty. Coordinators need to develop clear policies on the required boundaries to prevent, to the extent they can, dilemmas from arising due to inappropriate boundaries in inevitable dual relationships (Brown et al., 2014).

Gate Keeping

Gate keeping is a fundamental ethical and professional responsibility of all counseling faculty, not just supervisors (Bernard & Goodyear, 2019). Gatekeeping truly begins in the admission process and never ceases until the student graduates. Gatekeeping should be central to an academic program's philosophy, with clear expectations, accessible procedures, and regular dialogue (Hensley et al., 2003). Faculty must help students understand their professional duties and reporting requirements, modeling supportive approaches so gatekeeping is seen as a form of professional responsibility rather than punishment (Foster & McAdams, 2009). As we discuss in the chapter on assessment and evaluation, faculty, the coordinator, and university supervisor are deliberate in their assessment processes to determine "readiness" as it applied to each stage of the counseling program and fieldwork process.

Effective gatekeeping in counselor education means creating open, transparent communication between students and faculty. Ongoing dialogue ensures students understand evaluation criteria, processes, and their roles (Foster & McAdams, 2009). Clear standards, consistent policies, and accessible documentation support this. Faculty should encourage balanced communication, helping students and faculty build trust and a shared understanding of assessment (McAdams et al., 2007).

Foster and McAdams (2009) highlight that faculty members often experience a range of emotions and challenges when addressing poor performance in counselor education programs. They may feel a strong responsibility to uphold professional standards and ensure that students are adequately prepared for future roles. Yet, this responsibility can be accompanied by discomfort and reluctance, particularly when confronting students about deficiencies (Foster & McAdams, 2009). University supervisors may worry about the impact on their relationships with students and the potential consequences for students' academic and professional futures (Bernard & Goodyear, 2019). Additionally, ensuring consistent and transparent performance assessments can be difficult; faculty value fairness but may struggle to apply standards evenly, leading to uncertainty about the appropriate level of intervention (Hensley et al., 2003).

Regarding students, they can feel resentment toward their impaired classmates, whose difficulties can lead to extra work and lost opportunities for others (Foster & McAdams, 2009). They also express frustration toward university supervisors when they perceive them as ignoring or delaying addressing these impairments (McAdams et al., 2007). This lack of clarity and consistency in addressing performance issues can lead to mixed feelings about the professional performance review process. Students often do not understand the need for the process or how it is implemented, and they are not convinced that faculty members are aware of or address problems consistently (Hensley et al., 2003).

Transparency and communication are critical but challenging aspects of gatekeeping. A climate of openness and transparency in professional performance assessment is essential for students to trust the process and understand their role in it (Foster & McAdams, 2009). However, achieving this requires ongoing and uncensored dialogue between students and faculty members, which can be difficult to maintain. Students need ample opportunities for regular exchange with faculty members regarding evaluative criteria and the assessment process. Without this transparency, students may feel isolated, marginalized, and unsafe in speaking freely about their experiences and concerns, further complicating the gatekeeping process (Bernard & Goodyear, 2019; Foster & McAdams, 2009). Table 9.1 provides a chart for essential steps in gatekeeping.

TABLE 9.1 Essential Steps for Ethical and Effective Gatekeeping

Category	Key Points
Admission and Initial Assessment	Establish clear criteria and procedures for admission; Communicate expectations regarding professional readiness; Initiate assessment of student competence and suitability for the program
Ongoing Evaluation and Documentation	Conduct regular and deliberate assessments of student progress; Document performance, concerns, and interventions; Gather relevant data and evidence when issues arise; Encourage open dialogue about performance criteria and evaluation processes
Transparent Communication	Maintain clear, accessible standards and procedures for performance evaluation; Foster ongoing, uncensored dialogue between students and faculty; Ensure students understand their roles, responsibilities, and reporting requirements; Model supportive communication and address issues openly to build trust
Ethical Decision-Making	Apply ethical decision-making models (e.g., ACA Code of Ethics); Meet with supervisors or coordinators to develop growth plans and monitor outcomes; Remove students or interns from field sites, when necessary, based on severity of issues
Faculty Responsibilities	Recognize gatekeeping as a shared responsibility among all faculty and supervisors; Balance fairness, consistency, and transparency when assessing performance; Address poor performance with empathy and professionalism; Prepare for and manage potential emotional challenges associated with gatekeeping

(Continued)

TABLE 9.1 Continued	
Category	**Key Points**
Student Support and Engagement	Provide students with opportunities to discuss evaluation criteria and processes; Promote understanding of the necessity and implementation of performance reviews; Address student concerns regarding fairness and consistency; Reduce feelings of resentment or frustration through open communication and clear policies
Policy and Training	Develop clear policies on boundaries and dual relationships in training settings; Integrate gatekeeping content into orientation and supervisor training; Regularly review and update gatekeeping processes to reflect best practices

Remediation Plans

Remediation plans serve as a fundamental aspect of any counseling training program, designed to support students when their performance does not meet the expected standards (Klemashevich, 2021; Oliver et al., 2011). Remediation processes are a part of the larger programmatic structure, and we will focus on the process a coordinator and university supervisor can consider. Counseling research provides nuanced perspectives on effective remediation, emphasizing ethical responsibility, individualized approaches, and the fostering of interns' growth (Henderson et al., 2009; Kress & Protivnak, 2009). Remediation plans may be a result of ongoing issues or an issue that has arisen at any point in the fieldwork phase. In either case, they should be an opportunity for growth and not punitive (ACA, 2014). Use of a remediation plan ensures interns engage in learning that will support their use of ethical and legally sound behaviors, ultimately protecting client welfare (Henderson et al., 2009; Gaubatz & Vera, 2002).

Determining to Remediate

In the fieldwork phase there are obvious reasons for remediation: illegal behaviors, causing client harm, failure to uphold ethical standards, not meeting performance standards, and failure to complete academic tasks. There are also a wide variety of unethical behaviors that can arise that will prompt university supervisors and coordinators to consider remediation. We strongly recommend using the 2014 ACA *Code of Ethics*, relevant codes of ethics for the professional identity of the students, legal statutes, program determined learning outcomes and dispositions and chosen evaluation tools to guide conversations when the situation is not as obvious.

As we have espoused many times, interns need to be informed early about the standards, expectations, and evaluation procedures (Kaslow et al., 2007; ACA, 2014). When issues arise, whether continuously or suddenly, students need proactive communication individually and with the appropriate stakeholders (faculty, coordinators, and site supervisors). Feedback should be gathered from multiple sources and from all parties involved in a situation. Collaboration is encouraged to focus on encouragement and identifying resources to lead toward improvement (Henderson et al., 2009; Kress & Protivnak, 2009). Coordinators and university supervisors need to keep detailed records of observed issues, feedback provided, and responses from all parties involved. Consultation should be objective and focused on holistically understanding the situation, identifying any corrective measure already taken, and on determining the legal and ethical obligations in the situation. Lastly, coordinators and supervisors must be careful to avoid bias and discrimination to maintain fair posterity (Frame & Stevens-Smith, 1995).

Best Practices in Remediation

Remediation plans should be individualized, clear, and measurable (Falender & Shafranske, 2017) as Milne and Reiser (2017) recommend using SMART goals: Specific, Measurable, Achievable, Relevant, and Time-bound. Additionally, interns should have the opportunity to collaborate on the plan to foster ownership and empowerment. Within the written document, Kaslow and colleagues (2007) recommend the following details within the plan:

- Specific areas of concern
- The standards or competencies not met
- Objectives for improvement
- Actions or interventions required
- Support and resources available
- Methods and timelines for assessment
- Possible outcomes (successful completion, extension, or potential termination)

Remediation strategies can reflect evidence-based practices such as skill building work, additional supervision sessions, continued education and professional development, simulated counseling (Fouad et al., 2009), mentoring, and self-reflection work. The plan should also detail when meetings will occur to check in and assess progress. The plan should be monitored to changes and adaptations as benchmarks and growth items are achieved. If the plan is unsuccessful, coordinators and university supervisors need a plan in place for escalating the process to either include higher authorities or terminate. Remediation involves navigating complex interpersonal dynamics and institutional requirements. Intern resistance is a common challenge but can often be mitigated through empathetic communication, clarification of intentions, and encouragement (Johnson & Stewart, 2005). Supervisors should validate interns' feelings while maintaining accountability. Additionally, supervision teams must remain vigilant against bias by reviewing remediation decisions collaboratively, and best practices include peer review or consultation with independent advisors (Bernard & Goodyear, 2019). Resource constraints, such as limited time or specialized support, can also impact the process; therefore, institutions should plan for flexibility, ensuring that interns have access to additional training and supervision when needed (Elman & Forrest, 2007).

A dominant theme in the counseling literature is the importance of cultivating a supportive, growth-oriented training environment where remediation is destigmatized and embraced as an opportunity for professional development (Russell & Petrie, 1994). Key recommendations emphasize early intervention to address concerns proactively, minimizing their severity and promoting positive outcomes (Kaslow et al., 2007). Open communication between interns, supervisors, and program directors is essential, as is the flexibility to tailor remediation plans to individual needs and respond thoughtfully to intern feedback. Transparency remains crucial—expectations, processes, and potential consequences should be clearly communicated (American Counseling Association, 2014)—and thorough documentation at every stage ensures accountability and supports the integrity of the remediation process.

Tables 9.2 and 9.3 provide a checklist and decision-making matrix for determining remediation.

TABLE 9.2 Remediation Decision-Making Checklist

Identification of Performance or Conduct Concerns

Documentation and Assessment

Impact Evaluation

Communication and Due Process

Decision to Initiate Remediation

Table 9.3 Decision-Making Matrix for Determining Remediation

Area of Concern	Severity	Frequency	Impact on Stakeholders	Documentation	Supervisor Consultation	Recommended Action
Performance or Conduct	Minor	Isolated	Low	Noted, minimal	Optional	Monitor and provide feedback
Performance or Conduct	Moderate	Occasional	Moderate	Documented patterns	Recommended	Initiate remediation plan
Performance or Conduct	Severe	Frequent or ongoing	High (client risk or program integrity)	Thorough documentation	Required	Immediate remediation or removal consideration
Legal/Ethical Violation	Any	Any	High	Comprehensive	Required, consult ethics/legal counsel	Immediate intervention, possible removal

Decision-Making in Removing an Intern from a Counseling Program

The decision to remove an intern from a counseling program is a significant and complex process, requiring careful consideration of ethical standards, thorough documentation, and established remediation procedures. This process should be anchored in clear and accessible performance standards, with articulated consequences presented at the beginning of the training program (Elman & Forrest, 2007). Clearly defined remediation and dismissal policies—outlined in program handbooks—ensure both fairness and transparency for all involved.

Transparency in performance assessment is vital to maintaining a climate of trust and accountability. Foster and McAdams (2009) highlight the importance of open communication and active student involvement in decisions related to gatekeeping. When concerns about an intern's conduct or performance surface, supervisors are responsible for developing structured remediation plans. These plans should specify clear goals, provide supportive measures, and include meticulous documentation at every stage (Elman & Forrest, 2007; Brown et al., 2014).

The primary focus in such decisions must always be the protection of clients and the upholding of professional standards (Brown et al., 2014). If an intern's actions involve legal or ethical violations, immediate intervention is required. In such cases, supervisors should consult with ethics and legal counsel to ensure appropriate and lawful handling of the situation (American Counseling Association, 2014). Comprehensive documentation and open communication are essential to support a climate of transparency. Interns should be consistently informed of the process, potential consequences, and afforded opportunities to respond to any concerns (Foster & McAdams, 2009).

Effective supervision, as described by Falender and Shafranske (2017), involves evaluating interns against clearly established competency benchmarks (Fouad et al., 2009). All concerns must be thoroughly documented to support fair and ethical decision-making throughout the process. If remediation efforts are unsuccessful, or the severity of the violation necessitates it, removal of the intern may be both appropriate and ethical to safeguard clients, maintain professional standards, and protect the integrity of the training environment (Brown et al., 2014).

Ultimately, the process of removing an intern from a counseling program must reflect best practices—upholding fairness, ethical responsibility, and transparency. Any removal should be managed with empathy,

TABLE 9.4 Decision-Making Guide for Removing an Intern

Issue Level	Risk to Clients/ Program	Documentation Required	Remediation Attempt	Consultation Needed	Action Steps	Ethical/Legal Considerations	Intern Involvement
Low (Minor Performance Concerns)	Minimal	Basic notes; formative evaluations	Yes, initial remediation plan	Consult supervisor	Provide feedback; monitor progress	Follow program policies	Intern notified, opportunity to respond
Moderate (Repeated Performance Issues)	Moderate	Detailed documentation; formal evaluations	Yes, structured remediation with goals/supports	Supervisor, faculty, possibly ethics/HR	Monitor closely; revise or extend remediation	Transparency, fairness	Intern participates in planning, feedback cycle
High (Serious Ethical or Legal Violation)	High/ Immediate	Comprehensive, chronological documentation	Attempted if appropriate, but may be by passed for severe infractions	Consult ethics/ legal counsel immediately	Immediate intervention; possible removal from program	Adhere to ACA Code of Ethics, legal mandates	Intern informed of process and rights

offering guidance about future options and demonstrating the program's commitment to fairness (Elman & Forrest, 2007).

Table 9.4 features a decision-making chart, provided as a reference for evaluating intern infractions. Coordinators and university supervisors should recognize that while some infractions—such as legal and ethical violations—are clear, others may require more discernment. Therefore, it is important to engage in careful deliberation when developing dispositions and key performance indicators (KPIs) as part of comprehensive program development. When issues regarding clinical skills, professional behaviors, or competency scale deficiencies arise and the situation is less clear, dispositions and KPIs can aid in the decision-making process.

Legal Considerations Outside of the Counseling Program

Counseling training programs may consider, as a part of larger program development, policies related to legal infractions committed by students prior to, or concurrently with their studies. Prior to beginning fieldwork and during fieldwork, programs can collect background checks, fingerprints, or other information related to legal histories of interns. While some fieldwork sites, such as those with minor clients or protected populations, might also collect this information, programs should consider their own screening procedures. We encourage consulting with legal experts about what information may be collected and at which points in time it can be collected. Additionally, programs should consult on what rights and capabilities they have when legal infractions committed by interns.

Conclusion

Fieldwork coordinators and university supervisors are tasked with ensuring interns uphold ethical and legal standards during their counseling training programs, in the fieldwork phase, and outside of the program. While there will be situations where violations are clear, there are situations that can be more subjective in nature. Most important in the gatekeepers role is to have established procedures, decision-making criteria, continuous assessment, and plans in place for when an objective of subjective situation arises.

Bibliography

American Counseling Association. (2014). *ACA code of ethics*. Alexandria, VA: Author.

Bernard, J. M., & Goodyear, R. K. (2019). *Fundamentals of clinical supervision* (6th ed.). Boston, MA: Pearson.

Borders, L. D., & Brown, L. L. (2005). *The new handbook of counseling supervision*. Mahwah, NJ: Lawrence Erlbaum Associates.

Borders, L. D., Brown, L. L., & Purgason, L. L. (2014). Triadic supervision with practicum and internship counseling students: A peer supervision approach. *Counselor Education and Supervision, 53*(2), 146–160.

Brown, C., Murdock, N. L., & Abela, A. (2014). Ethical issues associated with training in university counseling centers. *Training and Education in Professional Psychology, 8*(4), 269–276.

Council for Accreditation of Counseling and Related Educational Programs (CACREP). (2024). *2024 Standards*. Retrieved from https://www.cacrep.org/for-programs/2024-cacrep-standards/

Elman, N. S., & Forrest, L. (2007). Remediation and dismissal policies in counseling psychology training programs: Necessary components. *The Counseling Psychologist, 35*(6), 794–814.

Falender, C. A., & Shafranske, E. P. (2007). Competence in competency-based supervision practice: Construct and application. *Professional Psychology: Research and Practice, 38*(3), 232–240.

Falender, C. A., & Shafranske, E. P. (2017). *Supervision essentials for the practice of competency-based supervision*. Washington, DC: American Psychological Association.

Foster, V. A., & McAdams, C. R. (2009). A framework for creating a climate of transparency for professional performance assessment: Fostering student investment in gatekeeping. *Counselor Education and Supervision, 48*, 271–284.

Fouad, N. A. et al. (2009). Competency benchmarks: A model for understanding and measuring competence in professional psychology across training levels. *Training and Education in Professional Psychology, 3*(4), 5–26.

Frame, M. W., & Stevens-Smith, P. (1995). Out of harm's way: Enhancing monitoring and dismissal processes in counselor education programs. *Counselor Education and Supervision, 35*(2), 118–129.

Gaubatz, M. D., & Vera, E. M. (2002). Do formalized gatekeeping procedures increase programs' follow-up with deficient trainees? *Counselor Education and Supervision, 41*(4), 294–305.

Henderson, A. et al. (2009). Creating supportive clinical learning environments: An intervention study. *Journal of Clinical Nursing, 19*, 177–182.

Hensley, L. G., Smith, S. L., & Thompson, R. W. (2003). Assessing competencies of counselors-ln-training: Complexities In evaluating personal and professional development. *Counselor Education and Supervision, 42,* 219–230.

Johnson, W. B., & Stewart, D. W. (2005). Best practices in graduate student remediation: Lessons learned from psychology training programs. *Professional Psychology: Research and Practice, 36*(4), 369–375.

Kaslow, N. J. et al. (2007). Guiding principles and recommendations for the assessment of competence in professional psychology. *Professional Psychology: Research and Practice, 38*(5), 441–451.

Kaslow, N. J., & Rice, D. G. (2013). Promoting ethical practice in supervision. *Training and Education in Professional Psychology, 7*(4), 229–236.

Klemashevich, J. M. (2021). An integrative approach to the remediation of student trainees in Christian counseling programs. *Journal of Psychology and Christianity, 40*(3), 237–246.

Kress, V. E., & Protivnak, J. J. (2009). Professional development plans to remedy problematic counseling student behaviors. *Counselor Education and Supervision, 48*(3), 154–166.

Lambie, G. W., & Sias, S. M. (2009). Ethical issues in supervision. In G. R. Waltz, J. C. Bleuer, & R. K. Yep (Eds.), *Counselor's desk reference* (2nd ed., pp. 103–108). New York, NY: Springer Publishing Company.

McAdams, C. R., III, & Foster, V. A. (2007). A guide to just and fair remediation of counseling students with professional performance deficiencies. *Counselor Education and Supervision, 47,* 2–13.

McAdams, C. R., III, Foster, V. A., & Ward, T. J. (2007). Remediation and dismissal policies in counselor education: Lessons learned from a challenge in federal court. *Counselor Education and Supervision, 46,* 212–229.

McCarthy, A. K., & Archer, J. (2021). Effective supervision in counselor education: Current approaches and best practices. *Journal of Counseling & Development, 99*(1), 45–54.

Milne, D. L., & Reiser, R. P. (2017). *A manual for evidenced-based CBT supervision.* Hoboken, NJ: Wiley.

Oliver, R. M., Wehby, J. H., & Reschly, D. J. (2011). Teacher classroom management practices: Effects on disruptive or aggressive student behavior. *Campbell Systematic Reviews, 4* (1–56).

Remley, T. P., & Herlihy, B. (2020). *Ethical, legal, and professional issues in counseling* (6th ed.). Upper Saddle River, NJ: Pearson.

Russell, R. K., & Petrie, T. A. (1994). Issues in training effective supervisors. *Applied & Preventive Psychology, 3*(1), 27–42.

Stoltenberg, C. D., & McNeill, B. W. (2010). *Counselor supervision: An integrated developmental model* (3rd ed.). New York, NY: Routledge.

Welfel, E. R. (2015). *Ethics in counseling & psychotherapy* (5th ed.). Boston, MA: Cengage Learning.

Index

Note: **Bold** page numbers refer to tables.